ABOUT THE AUTHORS

His Holiness the Dalai Lama is the spiritual leader of the Tibetan people. He has resided in exile in Dharamsala, India, since 1959 when Chinese forces invaded Tibet. His tireless efforts on behalf of world peace and human rights have brought him international recognition, including the Nobel Peace Prize in 1989.

Dr Howard Cutler runs a psychiatric practice in Phoenix, Arizona. He first met the Dalai Lama in 1982 while visiting India on a research grant to study Tibetan Medicine.

Also by His Holiness the Dalai Lama

The Art of Happiness (with Howard C. Cutler)
The Essence of Happiness (with Howard C. Cutler)
An Open Heart
The Transformed Mind

The ART of HAPPINESS at Work

HIS HOLINESS
THE DALAI LAMA

and

HOWARD C CUTLER, MD

Hodder & Stoughton

First published in Great Britain in 2003 by Hodder and Stoughton
A division of Hodder Headline

A Mobius book

1 3 5 7 9 10 8 6 4 2

A CIP catalogue record for this title is
available from the British Library

Hardback ISBN 0 340 83119 7
Trade paperback ISBN 0 340 83317 3

Printed and bound in Great Britain by
Clays Ltd, St Ives plc

Hodder and Stoughton
A division of Hodder Headline
338 Euston Road
London NW1 3BH

AUTHOR'S NOTE

In this book, extensive conversations with the Dalai Lama have been recounted. The Dalai Lama generously allowed me to select whatever format for the book I felt would most effectively convey his ideas. I felt that the narrative format found in these pages would be most readable and at the same time impart a sense of how the Dalai Lama incorporates his ideas into his own daily life. With his approval, I organized this book according to subject matter, and in doing this, I have chosen to combine and integrate material that may have been taken from several different conversations. The Dalai Lama's skilled interpreter, Dr. Thupten Jinpa, kindly reviewed the final manuscript to assure that there were no inadvertent distortions of the Dalai Lama's ideas as a result of the editorial process.

A number of case histories and personal anecdotes have been presented to illustrate the ideas under discussion. In order to maintain confidentiality and protect personal privacy, in every instance I have changed names and altered details and distinguishing characteristics to prevent identification of particular individuals.

CONTENTS

INTRODUCTION

Toward the end of 1998, *The Art of Happiness: A Handbook for Living* was published, and to my complete surprise the book rapidly gained widespread popularity. For some reason, the Dalai Lama's simple messages seemed to resonate in the hearts of millions of readers:

- The purpose of life is happiness.
- Happiness is determined more by the state of one's mind than by one's external conditions, circumstances, or events—at least once one's basic survival needs are met.
- Happiness can be achieved through the systematic training of our hearts and minds, through reshaping our attitudes and outlook.
- The key to happiness is in our own hands.

The book's success had been as unexpected to the Dalai Lama as to myself. In fact, he had been only vaguely aware of the book's popularity when I met with him one afternoon, after the book had already been on *The New York Times* bestseller list for several months. As a Buddhist monk, the Dalai Lama was unconcerned with issues such as book sales; in fact, his monastic training strictly prohibits the pursuit of fame or money, so he had paid little attention as the book climbed bestseller lists around the world. When I informed him about the book's success, he seemed genuinely surprised. "Really?" he asked. I assured him it was true. As this was his first visit to the United States since publication of *The Art of Happiness,* and because of the book's high profile, I anticipated the possibility of questions by the media. So I thought that I had better debrief him. After all, this was just one among dozens of books by him that had come out over the years. I had visions of him appearing on a program like *Larry King Live,* being asked about the book, and his replying "The art of *what* . . . ?" This did in fact happen to a lesser degree when he appeared on that very program and King asked him, "Why an *art*?" The Dalai Lama had no idea. The publisher had chosen the title. Since he had graciously left the final structure and editing of the book up to me, I asked him if he had any questions about the book. He had just one question: "Has the book been helpful for people?" he asked.

"Oh, yes. Absolutely," I assured him enthusiastically.

For the first time, he seemed to take an interest. "In what way?" he asked with genuine curiosity.

He caught me off guard on that one. "Uh, er . . . I dunno . . . ," I stammered, shrugging my shoulders. Although the publisher had passed along many moving letters from readers describing how the book had helped them, at that moment I couldn't think of a single example. Finally, I mumbled some response, I don't remember what, feeling a bit like a college student bluffing my way through an oral exam.

Later, however, I reflected on his question. It was impossible to really know the extent to which his ideas may have helped others, but I wondered if these ideas had had an impact on me. Clearly they had. After having spent countless hours with him and five years crafting our first book, was I any happier? Yes. *Definitely,* I thought, smiling to myself as I echoed his response to me many years earlier, after I had asked him if he was happy. Still, I felt that there must be more. While I felt that his ideas had helped me become a happier person, I still had a long way to go before achieving the kind of pervasive joy that he seemed to radiate so effortlessly. And I wanted to make that journey.

So, I found that there were still gaps and unanswered questions. I began wishing for an opportunity to sit down with him again, refine our previous discussions, add new twists and topics, deepen our discussion about leading a happy life in this complex world. And the questions were not mine alone. Since publication of our book, I had heard from many people, friends and strangers, pointing out missing pieces, voicing questions, spotting topics that were left out of our book. Along with these questions came numerous conversations that began with, "Hey, Howard, if you ever have a chance to talk with the Dalai Lama again, could you please ask him about . . . ?" It wasn't long before the idea of a second book began to take shape.

Of course, there was a major roadblock to considering another book. As the years have gone by and the Dalai Lama's role on the world stage has grown, there have been escalating demands on his schedule. He simply might not have the time. Not to mention that there were more important things for him to do. I worried that he might not agree to it, that he wouldn't be able to find the time. Still, I knew his Achilles' heel, his secret weakness, one that I was prepared to exploit shamelessly—his sincere wish to be of service to others. It is well known among those close to him that the Dalai Lama has a hard time saying no to any project if he feels that it would be of some benefit to others. And in making my request, I knew that if all else failed, he is susceptible to whining.

Fortunately, it didn't take much whining. Once convinced that there would be some benefit to others by our meeting, he readily agreed, and so we found ourselves together once again at his home in Dharamsala, India, preparing to begin work on a sequel to *The Art of Happiness.*

Our first book had focused on the general theme of inner development. But, as was pointed out to me by many readers, an individual does not live in a vacuum. We live in the world, interact with society, and the society we live in can clearly have an impact on the individual. So, we began by mapping out a course of action, preparing a list of the topics that we had omitted from our first book. It quickly became clear that in our first book we had avoided any in-depth discussion of problems in society. There was a reason for that. As I pointed out in our first book, by inclination as well as by training as a psychiatrist, I had always confined my field of interest to exploring the inner workings of the mind, the human psyche. I was always fascinated with inner dynamics, how various destructive emotions arose and manifested in the lives of individuals. Discussion of the wider issues of society held little interest for me. And besides, the myriad problems in society seemed so vast, so overwhelming, so daunting, that my reaction was simply to block them out. Denial, that ol' standby defense mechanism. A popular favorite. While I was no longer practicing individual psychotherapy, I could well remember sessions when the patient would start talking about her or his job worries, money problems, finances, living in a violent world, and my mind would immediately begin to wander. It wasn't that these issues were not legitimate sources of the patient's suffering, but these problems seemed so solutionless that I simply felt helpless. And so as soon as a patient began talking about these issues, my eyes would glaze over as a kind of invisible film descended over my mind. I comforted myself by reasoning that since there was nothing I could do about these things, there was no way for me to help. I even remember feeling vaguely offended, put out, when patients brought up these issues in therapy—*Hey, that's not my job!* Couldn't they understand that?

During the discussions that led to our first book, the Dalai Lama had often brought up global issues and problems in society. But I had always managed to slip away, redirect him, and bring the discussion back to the level of the individual. Yet here we were, confronting the bigger picture once again. The list of topics we were developing was legion: violence, fear for the safety of ourselves and our families, racism and intolerance, poverty, pollution and destruction of the environment, the disintegration of the family, growing old in a youth-oriented culture, dwindling financial and personal resources, corporate greed and scandals, unemployment, widespread job dissatisfaction. The list went on and on. If we were to explore all facets of the human experience, have a holistic approach to human suffering and happiness, there was no way that we could avoid facing these problems head-on. In the post–9/11 world and the post-Enron economy, these issues loomed larger than ever.

There was another factor that still made me hesitate to address these topics, a factor that I brought up early in our discussions. Raising my concern to the Dalai Lama, I explained, "I know that we are going to be talking about problems in society. And I'm really eager to know what you think. You've mentioned in the past that you identify most strongly with your role as a Buddhist monk, and I've attended enough of your Buddhist teachings to know the depth of your scholarship in Buddhist philosophy. But after knowing you for so many years, I think you're well qualified to discuss many other fields. I know you're a firm believer in the importance of ethical values, basic human values. And many times I've heard you speak passionately about applying these ethical values to every field of human endeavor—business, politics, economics, and so on. But over the years, I've seen you meet not only with religious figures from every major tradition, but also with leaders in every field—the world political leaders, top scientists, business leaders—and engage in dialogues and conferences with them." He nodded his head in agreement as I spoke. "In essence, you've gained a great practical education by intensive discussion with experts in many fields, and you've thought a great deal about incorporating these religious ideals . . ."

"More from the side of secular ethics," he corrected.

"From the perspective of secular ethics, then," I allowed. "But the point I'm getting at is that I don't think I'm qualified to be discussing these things with you. I was trained in psychiatry, medicine before that, and art before that. I barely even watched the news, at least not until September eleventh. In fact, I'm probably the least qualified person to be exploring these topics with you."

The Dalai Lama was silent for a moment while he considered what I said, then responded, "These human problems, these problems in society don't appear from nowhere. They are created by human beings, and arise from the same problems all individuals have; but collectively, on a wider scale, there is an additive effect. But as a psychiatrist I think you are qualified to understand the psychological factors that contribute to the individual destructive behaviors—behaviors that then create problems in society when large groups of people act in certain ways. And besides," he added, "you are a human being. You live in the world like anyone else. You don't need to be an expert to discuss these things. If these problems in society are to get better, it is not enough that a few experts discuss these things. Every individual has to change, and the only way to do this is for ordinary people to have greater awareness of the bigger problems, an understanding of what creates the problem, and a desire to change things person by person. So, as a member of society you are as qualified as anyone else. And the only way to change is through education. So if we raise certain questions as we discuss things, then you can read, research, learn about these things. Find your own examples. That is up to each of us. That's our responsibility."

And so we began. As our discussions progressed over the next couple of years, it became clear that the subject of human happiness was so vast and there were so many topics to cover that we would need to divide the material up into several books. But the question remained: How should we structure and present the material? And where should we begin? With little deliberation, the logical choice seemed clear—in looking at the daily routine of most people, we would select the activity that takes up the bulk of our waking hours: work.

When I suggested work as the topic for our next book, to be titled *The Art of Happiness at Work,* the Dalai Lama readily agreed, and laughed. "Hmmm . . . *The Art of Happiness at Work.* You know, in my work I travel a lot, and I schedule a certain time to fly that is suitable for me, but then, delay, delay, delay!" He laughed harder. "I get a little irritation, a little 'unhappiness' in the workplace. So I think that maybe I need a special 'Art of Happiness' book too."

After some discussion, we came up with a structure for a series of books that will broaden the topics introduced in *The Art of Happiness: A Handbook for Living,* and offer a more comprehensive approach to the complex subject of human happiness. We begin with this second volume, on applying the Dalai Lama's ideas to find greater happiness at work. A future volume will expand on specific features of the workplace environment, explore how to bring ethics and basic human values into the world of business and commerce, and discuss leadership, showing how anyone can cultivate the qualities of an effective leader. Also, in a separate volume we will continue our exploration of how to incorporate ethical principles into daily life, and address the question, "How can we maintain happiness given the harsh realities of today's world?" That volume will touch upon some of the inevitable conditions of human existence, such as growing older, illness and dying, as well as some of the tough problems of today's world: violence, racism, poverty, destruction of the environment. It will explore how we can live without fear, and with courage and hope. The last volume of the series will add the final piece to our quest for happiness, showing how our unhappiness is ultimately caused by the gap between appearance and reality, the gap between how we perceive things and how things really are. We will trace the roots of our destructive emotions, the states of mind that create our suffering and obstruct our happiness, to distortions in thinking, our habitual misperceptions of ourselves, others, and the world around us. Thus, in our last volume we will return the focus to our inner world, as the Dalai Lama will weave together the concepts presented in the earlier works and present a practical structured program for inner development.

But now, to work . . .

Chapter 1

TRANSFORMING DISSATISFACTION AT WORK

It had been a long day for the Dalai Lama. Even by the time he had eaten his meager breakfast of *tsampa*[1] and tea at 7:30 A.M., he had already been up for four hours, completing his rigorous daily regimen of prayer, study, and meditation. After breakfast he began his usual workday, and that day there was a full line-up: meeting with one person after another, he saw an Indian government liaison officer, the head lama of one of the ancient lineages of Tibetan Buddhism, the president of a member republic of the Russian Federation, a high official in the Tibetan government-in-exile, and various members of his private office staff. And scheduled among these private meetings, I watched with admiration as he met with a group of newly arrived Ti-

[1] *Tsampa* is a traditional Tibetan staple food. It is made from roasted barley flour eaten in the form of a dryish dough mixed with tea.

betan refugees. They had made the arduous journey across the Himalayas by any means of conveyance they could find, lucky if they could afford a ride on an antediluvian bus, but more likely to have caught a lift, riding in the open bed of a shuddering pickup truck. Some had crossed the rugged border on foot, climbing high-altitude passes with grim determination. Here and there one could see a child missing a finger or a toe—casualties of frostbite. Many arrived penniless, destitute, their traditional *chubas* (native Tibetan costumes) tattered and dusty from the long journey. In some of the older faces, ruddy faces, weathered and creased by winds and harsh climate, one could detect traces of untold suffering, spirits hardened by years of mistreatment at the hands of the Chinese Communists. For many of these people, however, a mere glimpse of the Dalai Lama, the fulfillment of a lifelong dream, was enough to revive their withered spirits and infuse them with renewed hope and joy. He offered them all, young and old, words of hope and encouragement, as well as hardheaded practical advice, ranging from "Education is critical to success" to "Now you men should be careful of going with prostitutes—you could catch a disease."

Finally, it was 2 P.M., his last scheduled appointment for the day. And here was I. I had been allotted several hours each afternoon to collaborate on our book, and I was here to collect. Our meetings were far from chatty tête-à-têtes, however. In fact, I often gave him no end of difficulty as we struggled to reconcile East and West, pestering him with endless questions, a fair proportion of which he labeled so silly or impossible to answer that it had become a running joke between us, trying even his legendary patience.

Standing outside on his bougainvillea-draped porch, with the majestic snowcapped Dhauladhar Mountains of northern India as a backdrop, the Dalai Lama greeted me warmly as he led me inside his home. Little had changed in this room since our first meeting twenty years before. The same traditional Tibetan *thanka* paintings lined the pale yellow walls, the same Buddhist shrine covered with ornate Buddhist icons at one end of the room, and the same floor-to-ceiling relief map of Tibet dominating the opposite wall. Even the modest furniture appeared to be the same, although it's possible the sofa may have been reupholstered.

As I unpacked my notebooks and fumbled with my tape recorder, we spoke casually about some of his activities and meetings earlier that day. The Dalai Lama generally scheduled our meetings for his last appointment of the day, so as I loitered in the attached reception room waiting for our meeting to begin, I often had the opportunity to observe the collection of individuals who came to meet with him. On that day in particular I was struck by the diversity of individuals seeking his time and counsel, people coming to visit him from all corners of the earth.

Thinking about this as I began our session, I said, "You know, I couldn't help but notice how many different kinds of people come to see you, people with various professions, all sorts of jobs. And I was thinking about how you also are involved in so many different kinds of activities. Now, this week I want to focus on the topic of work . . ."

"Yes. Good." The Dalai Lama nodded.

"And since we're going to be talking about work this week, I was just curious, what do you consider to be your primary job?"

The Dalai Lama looked puzzled. "What do you mean?"

I was puzzled why he was puzzled. It seemed to be a simple question.

"Well, in the West," I explained, "when you meet somebody, often the first question you ask a stranger is, 'What do you do?' meaning specifically, 'What kind of work do you do? What's your job?' So, if you met a complete stranger and they didn't know you or had never heard of the Dalai Lama and they didn't even know what your monk's robes signified, they just met you as a human being and they asked you, 'What do you do for a living?' what would you tell them?"

The Dalai Lama reflected in silence for a long while, and finally declared, "Nothing. I do nothing."

Nothing? In response to my blank stare, he repeated himself. "If I was suddenly posed with this question that would probably be my answer. Nothing."

Nothing? I didn't buy it. He clearly worked as hard as anyone I knew, harder even. And as grueling as this day had been, it was light duty compared to his schedule during his frequent trips abroad. In fact, informally attached to his small staff on a speaking tour of the U.S. the year before, I had witnessed a remarkable display of relentless activity, dedication, and hard work: as a statesman, he had met with President George W. Bush, Secretary of State Colin Powell, and a host of high-ranking senators and members of Congress. As a teacher, an ordained Buddhist monk and consummate Buddhist scholar, he gave extensive lectures expounding the most subtle facets of Buddhist philosophy. As a Nobel Peace Prize laureate and tireless advocate for world peace and human rights, he gave public addresses to tens of thousands, hundreds of thousands. As a religious leader striving to promote interfaith dialogue and harmony, he met with religious figures from many faiths: priests, rabbis, ministers, and swamis, even the president of the Mormon Church. He met with scientists, scholars, entertainers, the famous and the obscure. And in each place he visited, he met with local Tibetan refugees struggling to make a life and prosper in their new country. He worked morning till night, traveling from city to city with such speed that one place seemed to merge into the next. And yet not a single meeting or event on this tour was initiated at his own request—all were based on invitations from others. And even more remarkable—no matter how rigorous his schedule became, he seemed to handle his work effortlessly. He was happy doing it.

He did nothing? Not by a long shot.

"No, really," I pressed. "What if someone persisted and asked you again?"

"Well," he laughed, "in that case, I would probably say, 'I just look after myself, just take care of myself.'" Perhaps sensing my frustration with this glib response, he smiled and continued, "I think maybe this answer isn't entirely serious. But actually, if you think about it, that's true. All six billion human beings in the world are just 'taking care of number one.' Isn't it?[2] So

[2] When speaking English, the Dalai Lama sometimes uses the expression *"Isn't it?"* to mean, *"Don't you agree?"* or *"Don't you think so?"*

whether one is a professional, or whatever line of work one is in, each of us from birth to death is just working to take care of ourselves. That's our main task."

My attempt to pin him down on his job description was getting nowhere fast. And this wasn't the first time I had noticed his natural reluctance to engage in discussion about his role in the world. Perhaps it was due to a certain lack of self-absorption, an absence of self-involvement. I don't know. But I decided to drop the subject of his job for now and turn to the wider issue.

"Well, in working to take care of ourselves most people need some kind of job. Now many times in the past I've heard you say that the purpose of life is happiness."

"That's right," he affirmed.

"So, we need a way to be happy at work as well as at home, but that's not always easy. Let me give you an example of a friend of mine. I gave her a copy of *The Art of Happiness* shortly after it came out. She told me that she kept it on her bedside table and read from it each night before she went to bed. She was tremendously inspired by your words, and she said that when she read it she felt it was really possible to be happy. But then she told me, 'When I go to bed, I'm thinking that if I make the effort, happiness is within my reach, genuine happiness is out there waiting for me. But then the next morning I have to get up at five o'clock in the morning and face an hour-long commute to work. And the minute I step into the office, everything changes—I have to deal with the pressures, the demands, my boss is a jerk, and I can't stand my co-workers. And suddenly it seems like the idea of happiness slips away. It just evaporates. Things are so hectic that I barely have a chance to catch my breath, let alone think about training my mind or inner development. And of course the company I work for doesn't care a bit about my happiness. But I need to work. I need the money. I can't just quit and expect to get another job. So, how can I find happiness at work?'

"And of course my friend isn't an isolated case," I continued. "In many countries throughout the world, there seems to be a kind of widespread dissatisfaction at work. In fact, I recently read a survey that reported that nearly half of American workers are dissatisfied at work, unhappy with their jobs. I've talked to some experts who say that the number may even be higher than that. And things seem to be getting worse. According to the Conference Board, the nonprofit organization that conducted the survey, that same survey showed that over the past five or six years the percentage of people who are satisfied with their job has dropped by around eight percent."

The Dalai Lama appeared surprised. "Why is that?" he asked.

"Well, according to the studies I've read, there may be a variety of reasons, ranging from inadequate compensation, or simple boredom, to more complex factors related to the specific nature of the work or the workplace conditions. There are all sorts of things that can make a person miserable at work: poor social atmosphere, lack of recognition, not enough variety, and other things. In fact, I'd be interested in hearing your opinion on each one of these factors. But let me give you an example. A few days before leaving for Dharamsala, I had dinner with some friends who were both in the software industry and worked for large corporations. They spent most of the dinner sitting around complaining about their jobs. Even though they worked for different companies, one thing they both mentioned was that they felt they had no control over what they did every day. They had no sense of autonomy, no freedom to do their work in their own way. They both complained that they didn't get enough information and direction from their bosses, but once they were finally given a clear-cut task or assignment, they wanted to carry out the assignment in their own way. Instead, the supervisor seemed to be standing over them breathing down their necks, giving them no room for creativity or personal initiative. They resented the fact that not only didn't they have any control over the kind of work they are required to do, they couldn't even choose how to go about doing it.

"So, do you have any thoughts about how a person could go about increasing their feeling of autonomy or freedom at work?"

"I don't know," the Dalai Lama responded. "Of course it will completely depend on the person's individual circumstances, what position they are in."

"Any general suggestions?"

He reflected for a moment. "Let's take the example of a prisoner. Now of course it is best not to be in prison, but even in that situation, where a person may be deprived of freedom, he or she may discover small choices that they are able to make. And even if somebody is in prison, with very rigid rules, they can undertake some spiritual practices to try to lessen their mental frustrations, try to get some peace of mind. So they can work on internal development. In fact, I've heard that there is a program here in India where prisoners are being taught meditation.

"So, I'm thinking that if people can do this under the extreme conditions of prison, in the workplace people may try to discover small things, small choices that they can make in how to go about their work. And of course, somebody may work on an assembly line with little variation in how to do their tasks, but they still have other kinds of choices in terms of their attitudes, how they interact with their co-workers, whether they utilize certain inner qualities or spiritual strengths to change their attitude at work even though the nature of the work may be difficult. Isn't it? So, perhaps that would help.

"Of course, when you are talking about rigid rules and lack of freedom, that doesn't mean that you are required to blindly follow and accept everything others tell you. In instances where the worker might be exploited, where the employer thinks of nothing but profit and pays a small salary and demands a lot of overtime, or where one may be asked to do things that are not appropriate or are unethical, one should not simply think, *Well, this is my karma,* and take no action. Here it is not enough to think, *I should just be content.*

"If there is injustice, then I think inaction is the wrong response. The Buddhist texts mention what is called 'misplaced tolerance,' or 'misplaced forbearance.' So, for example, in the case of Tibetans, in the face of Chinese injustice generally, misplaced patience or forbearance refers to the sense of endurance that some individuals have when they are subject to a very destructive, negative activity. That is a misplaced forbearance and endurance. Similarly, in the work environment, if there is a lot of injustice and exploitation, then to passively tolerate it is the wrong response. The appropriate response really is to actively resist it, to try to change this environment rather than accept it. One should take some action."

"What kind of action?" I asked.

"Of course it again depends on the situation," the Dalai Lama said reasonably. "But perhaps one could speak with the boss, with the management, and try to change these things."

"And if that doesn't work?"

"Then, revolt! Rebel!" He laughed. "This is what I generally say. One needs to actively resist exploitation. And in some cases, one may simply need to quit and to look for other work."

"Well, in today's world, exploitation certainly goes on," I agreed. "But in a lot of cases it isn't a matter of gross exploitation. It may just be that the nature of the job is very demanding. For example, when the economy is slow, companies are forced to cut back and lay off employees. Then the employees who are left have to take on more and more responsibility. Work becomes more stressful for those who remain. Any suggestions on how to cope more effectively with that type of situation, that sort of pressure or stress?"

"Of course it will vary from individual to individual how one emotionally and psychologically responds, and it also depends upon the nature of work and the nature of the company," he reminded me. "So there are many factors to take into account. For example, if you view your work as something that is really worthwhile—if, for instance, there is a higher purpose to your work—then of course, even if the work is very hard there may be a greater willingness to undergo that hardship. Under such circumstances you might think, *Oh, here's an opportunity to do something good for society.* So, it depends."

"But that kind of situation or attitude may not apply to everybody," I pointed out. "So, what I'm wondering about is a general approach to work overload, which is actually one of the other common sources of work dissatisfaction."

"What is this 'work overload,' what do you mean?" asked the Dalai Lama. The genuine curiosity in his voice suggested that he had never heard of the concept.

"Well, you know," I said, struggling for words, "where you are overloaded with work, and it becomes a source of stress."

"I still don't know what you mean by this term 'overload.' For example, your boss could give you some work which you could probably finish within a certain amount of time, but that's not overload because it is something you can accomplish, even if it is difficult. Or he could give you an amount of work that is impossible to finish in a certain amount of time, in which case you simply have to say 'I can't do this.' So, what do you mean?"

He wasn't getting it. But I failed to understand why he didn't get it. The concept of work overload isn't some obscure American custom, or even something unique to Western culture. After all, the Japanese have even coined the word *karoshi*—death by work overload. I decided to frame it in his terms. "Well, let's say you're a young monk and you're studying and practicing Buddhism. So your teacher would be the equivalent of your boss."

"O.K., right." He nodded. "I understand."

"And your job is to learn and memorize certain texts, so let's say your boss gives you a text that you need to memorize by next week. It's a very challenging text. Now, if you work hard, maybe you can memorize it by next week, but it's going to be very difficult. Then he comes back a few hours later and says, 'Well, now you have to memorize an additional text along with this text in the same amount of time.' And he's your boss—you can't just say, 'I'm going to quit, I'm not going to be a monk anymore.' So, work overload in this context means that you are given more and more to do but not enough time to do it."

"Oh, now I think I understand. For example, when I was around twenty, in Tibet, I had to give an important teaching, and for preparation I had homework early morning and late evening. Then I had to get up very early before my attendants arrived and even when my attendants had left, late into the evening I had to read and memorize. So I woke up a few hours earlier and went to bed a few hours later—that is the kind of overload?"

"Right."

"But then this is something that with extra attention and energy, it's something I could achieve. And that was O.K. for the short term. But if I were to continue with this having less sleep for a long time, having that kind of overload for a whole year, then it would be impossible."

"But that's the kind of thing many people are faced with these days," I informed him.

"So why can't these people say 'I can't do this' right from the beginning?" he asked. "Do they get fired?"

"In many cases, yes."

"In that case I think it goes back to knowing one's limitations. And if a boss gives more work to do and it is beyond their capacity, then I think they have to say something. They have to say 'This is too much work for me' and talk to the boss and try to reduce it. If that doesn't work, then they may need to look for new work.

"However, at that point let's say that the boss agrees to extra pay, and the employee agrees, then that is a person's decision and there's no cause to complain about overload. But if the boss gives too much work without increase of salary, then this 'overload' is just exploitation, the kind that we just spoke about.

"But I think in these kinds of situations, the employer has a responsibility to judge how much a person can reasonably be expected to do. Too much overload is simply a lack of concern, lack of respect. Even overloading an animal is disrespectful to that life—so, that's exploitation, it's unfair," he said with a resolute tone.

"I'm glad that you mentioned the issue of unfairness," I replied, "because that is another of the sources of workplace dissatisfaction. In fact, I think we're touching upon some of the most common sources of dissatisfaction at the workplace.

"In today's workplace environment, there's often a focus solely on production, productivity—produce, produce, produce. Now, this may be changing slowly, with more companies paying attention to creating a more humane environment, but in many cases the organization doesn't care about the personal welfare of the employees, or the inner state or satisfaction of the workers—all it cares about is the bottom line, making a bigger profit, keeping the share prices high. And this type of environment creates the conditions for all kinds of inequities, unfairness, stress for the employees, and so on. In view of that, how can we maintain a feeling of calmness and inner satisfaction in an environment that is focused only on production and profit?"

The Dalai Lama laughed. "Howard, some of your questions are so impossible! It is almost as if you are asking, 'How can beings in the hell realm learn to practice patience, tolerance, and tranquility?'

"There are not always easy answers. In modern society, you find many examples of unfairness—for example, corrupt leaders giving jobs or promotions to relatives instead of based on merit. These things are plenty. Now here, it's difficult to get satisfaction. How to deal with these things? That's a problem. Like in the Tibetan case, we're honest, we're not anti-Chinese, but the Chinese falsely accuse us of things and engage in bullying tactics in Tibet. Under those circumstances, legally they are wrong, we are right, but still we suffer. We're defeated. Under those circumstances, trying to get some satisfaction or some kind of peace of mind, now that's hard work.

"Millions of people are subjected to various forms of unfairness, isn't it? We need to fight against injustice outwardly, but at the same time we have to find ways to cope inwardly, ways to train our minds to remain calm and not develop frustration, hatred, or despair. That's the only solution. We may find help from our belief systems, whether we believe in karma or in God, but we can also use our human intelligence to analyze the situation and to see it from a different perspective. That will help," he said with conviction.

Referring to our many conversations over the years, I continued, "In the past, we've often spoken of training the mind as the key to happiness, and that one way to train our minds is to use our human intelligence, to use human reason and analysis to reshape our attitudes and outlook. In fact, this is a process which you've called 'analytic meditation.'"

"That's right," said the Dalai Lama.

"So, I'm wondering if you can take me through a specific example of this process. Let's say that we're going for a promotion at work, and we didn't get it. We're feeling really upset, we're feeling that it's unfair or we're jealous of the person who got the promotion. How do we deal with that?"

He replied thoughtfully, "It begins by deliberately analyzing whether responding with anger or jealousy, for instance, will benefit us or harm us in the long run. We have to deeply reflect on whether responding in this way brings a happier and more peaceful state of mind, or if those emotions serve to make us more unhappy. And we need to relate it to our own past experiences, thinking about the effect that these emotions have on our physical health, as well as our mental state. Think about times when you felt strong jealousy or hatred in the past and find out whether it made your life more satisfying or helped you achieve your goals. Think about how others responded to you when you were showing strong anger or jealousy, and analyze whether that helped you to have better relationships. So, think about these things until you are fully convinced of how damaging it is to ourselves to constantly respond to situations with hostility or jealousy, and how beneficial are the positive emotions like tolerance or contentment."

"O.K. Let's say that I'm convinced that it's destructive. Then what?"

"So, you are going for a new job or promotion, and you have the right qualifications, and you are worthy, but you didn't get the job. First you think, *Yes, I deserved that job,* but if you didn't get it you have a choice of how you will respond. You can be resentful and angry, but then you can think about how destructive that kind of mental state can be. That conviction alone will serve to make you more cautious of these emotions, and may reduce them a bit. So, don't keep thinking about the work you don't have. There will always be better jobs that you don't have. Don't continue to feel competitive or jealous. That only brings more worry, more dissatisfaction.

"But you still need a way to bring some kind of peace of mind. Here's where we need to use our capacity for critical thinking, for analysis. You begin by realizing that no situation is one hundred percent good or one hundred percent bad. Sometimes, particularly in the West, I've noticed a tendency to think in black-or-white terms. But in reality everything in life is relative. So, based on this reality, you can cultivate a wider perspective of the situation and try to see different angles. You can further analyze, realizing that with the better work and more money, that doesn't mean that you would have no problems. Some other jobs may have higher pay, but they come at a price, maybe longer hours or more responsibility and maybe risk of injury or other kinds of problems. In fact, if you really look at others in the higher positions, you may discover that there may be more demands, there may be more competition or jealousy from others. You might discover, for instance, that while your current work pays less, it may be easier in some ways, or even less dangerous in some instances.

"So, you continue to think about the reality, thinking, *Oh, yes that's my bad luck, I deserve that better job,* but since that didn't happen, instead of looking only at the lack of the better job, you could cultivate a wider perspective and see it from the other direction where you can think, *Well, yes, this may pay less and is not the best work, but since with this work I earn enough, a sufficient amount for my family and for my survival, I'm happy. It's* O.K. So, thinking along these lines, we can build contentment with our job even when things don't go our way."

The Dalai Lama paused and sipped some tea. "So," he continued, "I think through our own efforts, through cultivating a wider perspective, I think it is possible to become more content with our work."

"Of course, there's still so much widespread dissatisfaction with one's work," I mused. "I'm wondering if you have anything else to add here, any other ways we can look at things to . . ."

"Oh, definitely," he quickly replied. "Another way to build contentment, for example, is simply to reflect on how fortunate one is to have the work, how there are many people unable to get any kind of work. You can think, *There are other good things in my life, and I still have it better compared to many.* This is always the reality.

"Sometimes we forget that. We get spoiled. So, for example, in America there are many opportunities for employment. And there is also a large degree of freedom, and one's personal initiative can make a difference. With personal initiative one can advance. But at the same time there is still a lot of discontent and dissatisfaction with one's job. In other parts of the world, for example in countries like India and China, there are fewer opportunities open for employment. So, under such circumstances many individuals can't get jobs. But I've noticed that there the sense of satisfaction they derive from their job is much stronger and also they are more committed. In the same way, one can reflect on how much more difficult previous generations had it, going through world wars and so on. Sometimes we tend to forget these things, but if we think about it, this can increase our feeling of gratitude and contentment."

"Of course, you're right," I agreed. "I've also been to many countries, and I've seen coolies or baggage handlers here in India, or migrant farm workers, poor people working in rice paddies throughout Asia, or remote nomads in your own country, and many of these people seem genuinely happy and content. Of that there's no doubt. And I have to admit that we can become spoiled. But my country, America, was built on personal initiative. Shouldn't we want to advance, rather than just be content with the way things are?"

"Yes, Howard, but you shouldn't confuse contentment with complacency. You shouldn't mistake being content with one's job with just sort of not caring, not wanting to grow, not wanting to learn, just staying where one is even if one's situation is bad and not even making the effort to advance and to learn and to achieve something better. If we have a poor job, perhaps some unskilled labor, but we have the skills and qualifications for better work, by all means we should exert our best effort for the better work, make a good attempt. But if that fails, then instead of frustration, or becoming angry focusing only on the thought, *I tried but I wasn't able to make it*—then think, *O.K., I'll carry on with this work.* Be content with the work you have. So if you fail, that is where one's attitude and the practice of contentment can make the difference between anger, resentment, and frustration, and a calmer and happier attitude. That's where training of the mind comes in. These kinds of things, lines of reasoning, can diffuse your frustration and disturbance of mind. So contentment, I think, contentment—that's the key thing."

While he spoke, I thought about how difficult it might be for many people to adopt these lines of reasoning to diffuse their anger, hatred, and jealousy. I realized that is why he has so often stressed the fact that it isn't easy to train one's mind and reshape one's attitudes, that it takes repeated effort. And it takes time. For this kind of "analytical meditation" to work, one needs deep and sustained reflection on these alternative ways of viewing one's situation. One needs to be fully convinced of the absolute truth of this new perspective. Otherwise there is a danger of using these lines of reasoning merely as insincere rationalizations. A matter of "sour grapes." *Oh yeah? Well, I didn't want that job anyway!*. So, we're going for that promotion and we lose out. And we really wanted that promotion—every fiber of our being tells us that, even aside from the higher pay, the more important our job is, the happier we'll be.

So how do we convince ourselves beyond a reasonable doubt that the more important job may not necessarily make us happier? By looking at the evidence. By examining whether we're permanently happier from the last promotion we received or looking at people we know to see if those in a higher position are genuinely happier than those in a lower position. Or, we can look at the scientific evidence. In this case, for instance, while at SUNY Buffalo, Robert Rice, PhD, a prolific scholar in the field of job satisfaction, led a group that conducted a surprising study. Contrary to what one might expect, they found that those with more important jobs are no happier in life than those with less important jobs. This finding has been replicated in a number of similar wide-scale studies showing that while job satisfaction is linked with life satisfaction, the specific type of work one does, one's occupational prestige, or whether a person is blue collar or white collar, has little impact on one's overall life satisfaction.

There's an additional reason why it is sometimes a long and difficult process to reshape our attitudes and outlook, to change the habitual ways that we perceive the world, modify our customary interpretation and response to any given situation or event. What's the reason? When it comes down to it, many of us resist giving up our misery—a vexing and baffling feature of human behavior I often observed in the past when treating psychotherapy patients. As miserable as some people might be, for many there is a kind of perverse pleasure in the self-righteous indignation one feels when one is treated unfairly. We hold on to our pain, wear it like a badge, it becomes part of us and we are reluctant to give it up. After all, at least our characteristic ways of looking at the world are familiar. Letting go of our customary responses, as destructive as they may be, may seem frightening, and often that fear abides on a deeply ingrained subconscious level. And added to this, of course, are the secondary gains to holding on to our grudges, jealousy, and dissatisfaction, as our constant complaints serve to elicit sympathy and understanding from others. Or at least we think so, at least we hope so. Sometimes it works—our friends or co-workers join in with a catalogue of their own grievances, and a bonding takes place as we indulge in our own little festival celebrating life's inequities and the sins of our employers. Quite often, however, while our complaints may be received with outward expressions of sympathy, they may more likely be met with inward annoyance by those who have problems of their own to deal with.

Thinking about the difficulty of genuinely transforming our outlook and responding to these challenging situations in new ways, I remarked, "I think these are all good practical suggestions, although of course, even if these things are true, these lines of reasoning may not act as a consolation to everybody."

"That's true," the Dalai Lama admitted, "but my main point is that if there is a possibility to change your work environment, then of course you have the right to make that attempt. But you also need to understand the fundamental cause of various problems.

"So, once again, this brings us to the reality that everything is interconnected. If there are certain problems in the workplace, or layoffs and one is having difficulty finding a job, there are always many factors at play. So, you experience dissatisfaction. You suffer. Maybe some worldwide economic conditions or even some environmental problems may be at the root of the problem. In those cases, it does no good to take things so personally and complain to the company, or perhaps direct your anger toward one individual boss. And your anger could even turn into hatred, but even if your hatred escalates uncontrolled, and even if eventually you killed that person, it would have no effect on the situation, it would do nothing to change the wider problems.

"This kind of thing occurs, for example, in the Tibetan community here in India. There may be some people who are upset with the Tibetan government in exile, always complaining. So, focusing on some day-to-day activities of the government, they are dissatisfied, but they tend to forget that the government in exile is exactly that—an exiled government. And from that angle, the fundamental cause of the problem is the Chinese invasion and occupation of Tibet, which forced us into exile. That is the source of the problem. Once they focus on the real issue, it creates a sense of unity among us, which creates a sense of greater satisfaction instead of the divisions and conflicts caused when we lose sight of the wider issues and start bickering among ourselves.

"So, instead of just complaining and complaining, or directing your anger to a particular boss, in that type of situation, with your realization of the wider, more fundamental causes of the problem, it would be better if you redirected your thoughts. Think about the world, the global economy. Think about the environment. Look at the various forms of social injustice. Perhaps you could even make a small contribution to improve things in some way."

"Of course," I interjected, "there's often very little we can do to change these wider problems."

"That's true," the Dalai Lama conceded. "Your efforts may have little or no results, things may not change much. But at least instead of misplaced anger and frustration, you are transforming your mental energy, turning it in a more constructive direction. Your underlying motivation can change based on this wider perspective and it will build your enthusiasm to work, to make changes that will benefit society. Of course that takes time, but meantime if you can't change the work environment or the wider forces that contribute to the work environment, then you may need to change or adjust your outlook. Otherwise, you will remain unhappy at work and in your life."

Our meeting for the day was coming to a close, and thinking that he had finished, I began gathering up my notes, when he suddenly added a final comment about the harsh reality of life. Yet despite his unsentimental acknowledgment of life's difficulties, there was a certain fearlessness mingled with a gentle undertone of compassion in his voice.

"Now look. There will always be problems in life. It is just not possible to go through life without encountering problems. There is no event from which you get one hundred percent satisfaction, right? Some dissatisfaction will always remain. The better we are able to accept that fact, the better we will be able to cope with life's disappointments.

"So, take the example of a person who likes to eat sweet things, but doesn't like sour things. Then there is a certain kind of fruit that this person enjoys. That fruit may be mostly sweet, but it may also have a little bit of sourness in it. That person continues to enjoy the fruit, they don't stop eating it because it has a little sour taste. If they want to continue to enjoy eating that fruit, they have to accept the little bit of sourness in it. You can't separate the sweet from the sour in that piece of fruit; it is always going to be mixed. Life is just like that. As long as you are living, life will have good things but also some problems that you don't like. That's life."

So, life is tough. It seemed a grim truth upon which to be ending our meeting. And as if perfectly staged to underscore that dark note, at that moment there was a sudden crash of thunder and a deafening torrential downpour outside that muffled our words as we said goodbye. An instant later the electricity went off, an almost daily occurrence during this season in Dharamsala. The Dalai Lama was completely unruffled. In fact, his warm smile and cheerful manner were set off in bold relief against the darkened room and the ice storm raging outside. Clearly here was a happy man. Everything about him bespoke the possibility of leading a happy life despite life's inevitable troubles. He himself had weathered his fair share of problems, the loss of an entire nation as he was forced into exile as a result of the Communist Chinese invasion and occupation of Tibet. And he continued to tackle difficult problems on a daily basis—struggling to preserve his cultural heritage, fighting for the freedom of his people, for the human rights of all people. And often without success. Yet since the age of six, he had been engaged in the training of his mind, learning how to remain happy despite life's unavoidable adversities. It seems to have paid off.

So, he reminds us that if we can change some of the external conditions at the workplace that contribute to our dissatisfaction, we certainly should. If not, although it is always easy or quick, it is still possible to be happy at work through reshaping our attitudes and outlook, through inner training.

◆

Chapter 2

THE HUMAN FACTOR

In introducing the topic of work, I had told the Dalai Lama about my friend who had raised the question of how to practice the art of happiness at work. At the time she raised this question, I had asked her specifically what kinds of difficulties she was encountering.

"I don't know," she said, "there's just a lot of aggravation at work right now. And I'm getting it from two fronts, from my boss and also from some of my co-workers. My boss is way too demanding. He expects us to stay after hours and work even though we're not getting paid overtime, and he doesn't even appreciate it. He's rude and disrespectful. And I can't stand some of the other people at work, too. It's getting to the point where I almost dread going to work each day."

I asked my friend to tell me about the problem she was having with her co-workers, and she launched into a long convoluted tale of interoffice politics. Having no experience in her field, I couldn't make out much of what she said, but as far as I could understand, it had to do with a troublesome, backstabbing colleague who took over someone else's account and caused a rift among the employees as various factions formed in the department and aligned themselves into several camps. It sounded to me like an episode of the TV show *Survivor.*

In virtually every study of workplace conditions and the factors that contribute to employee satisfaction or dissatisfaction, the social climate of the organization plays a prominent role. Leading scholars in the emerging field of positive psychology, such as James Harter, Frank Schmidt, and Corey Keyes, in reviewing the existing literature on well-being at work, have found social interaction to be an important element in job satisfaction. Numerous researchers, including sociologist Karen Loscocco, while working at SUNY Albany, or Sheila Henderson conducting research at Stanford University, confirmed the key role of social atmosphere in employee satisfaction. In addition to providing greater satisfaction at the workplace, "work-related social support" was also found to be a factor in a person's general state of well-being.

It is of little surprise, therefore, that in our discussions about happiness at work, sooner or later we were bound to touch upon the subject of relationships at work—the human factor.

Resuming our conversation late the following afternoon, the Dalai Lama began, "There may be many factors or variables that affect the degree to which work contributes to happiness, and it depends on each individual's circumstances, make-up, and so on. Still, I think that in talking about work and happiness, there are some general things to keep in mind. I think it is important to remember that in all human activities, whether it is work or some other activity, the main purpose should be to benefit human beings. Now, what is it that we are seeking in our work, what is the purpose of work? Like any other human activity, we are seeking a sense of fulfillment and satisfaction and happiness. Isn't it? And if we are talking about human happiness, then of course human emotions come into play. So we should take special care to pay attention to the human relationships at work, how we interact with one another, and try to maintain basic human values, even at work."

"By 'basic human values,' you mean . . ."

"Just basic human goodness. Be a good person, a kind person. Relate to others with warmth, human affection, with honesty and sincerity. Compassion."

The Dalai Lama was still for several moments, as if deeply reflecting on these principles. It was remarkable. He had spent a lifetime speaking about these human values, repeating the same ideas over and over, yet each time he spoke of them it was with a certain freshness, as if he were discovering these concepts for the first time. He seemed to take great delight in speaking about human values, no matter how many times he had spoken of them before. So with a tone of genuine interest and enthusiasm, he resumed.

"You know, one thing that I think is crucial to keep in mind when talking about human values, compassion, and so on, is that these are not simply religious subjects. Compassion isn't something sacred, nor are anger and hatred considered to be profane just from a religious perspective. These things are important not because some religious text says so, but because our very happiness depends on them. These states of mind—compassion, human affection—have clear benefits to our physical health, our mental and emotional health, all of our relationships at work or at home, and are even critical for the ultimate benefit of society. They are for our own benefit. When we cultivate compassion, the primary beneficiary is really ourselves. After all, humans are social animals; we are built to work cooperatively with others for our survival. No matter how powerful a single person may be, without other human companions, that individual person cannot survive. And certainly, without friends he or she cannot lead a happy and fulfilling life. So, at work, if you have a warm heart, human affection, your mind will be calmer and more peaceful, which will give you a certain strength and also allow your mental faculties to function better, your judgment and decision-making abilities and so on."

A maroon-robed attendant silently glided into the room and poured some tea. He smiled. As I had observed in the past, there was no mistaking the atmosphere of mutual respect and affection between the Dalai Lama and his staff.

"I think on a basic level we are all human beings," he continued. "We all have the capacity to relate to one another with warmth, with affection, with friendship. So, if we are discussing happiness and satisfaction at work, like in all human activities, the human factor—how we relate to those around us, our coworkers, our customers, our boss—is of prime importance. And I think if we make a special effort to cultivate good relationships with people at work, get to know the other people, and bring our basic good human qualities to the workplace, that can make a tremendous difference. Then, whatever kind of work we do, it can be a source of satisfaction. Then you look forward to going to work, and you are happier there. You think, *Oh, I'm going to work to see my friends today!*" The Dalai Lama exclaimed with such an exuberant tone that I could almost picture him showing up at the factory, lunch pail in hand, greeting his co-workers this way. I couldn't help but smile.

"And this is something you can do yourself to improve your experience at work," the Dalai Lama went on. "Often, people wait for the other person to make the first move, but I think that is wrong. That is like when people remain neighbors for a long time but never get to know one another. So, you must take some initiative, even from your first day on the job, and try to show some friendship to others, introduce yourself, say hello, ask how long have you worked here, and so on. Of course, people will not always be receptive to that. In my own case sometimes I'll smile at someone, and that just makes them look upon me with greater suspicion." He laughed. "So people may have their own problems and frustrations, but then don't give up if they don't immediately respond. Try for one week, or one month. Eventually you may find others responding. Sometimes it's easy to give up, like sometimes I'm in a hotel or somewhere and I'll smile but the person ignores me. And if that remains their attitude, I'll assume the same attitude and ignore them." He chuckled. "I guess that's just human nature. But it shows how one person can influence another's attitude, which implies that even one person can make a big difference. One person can change the atmosphere of the workplace environment. You can see examples, for instance, of a very tense group of co-workers who don't get along, and then a new employee shows up, one who is warm and friendly, and after a while the mood and attitude of the whole group changes for the better. In the same way, sometimes you will see the opposite occur, where people at work are getting along and are friends, but then someone new will start work there, someone who is a troublemaker, and then that one can affect the whole group and cause conflicts and problems. So, each of us can have an effect on others, and even change the atmosphere at work. And in that respect, a low-level worker might have more impact on one's immediate surroundings at work, at least in one's department, than the boss.

"For example, I know some Tibetans who moved to Switzerland and went to work in factories there. And even without knowing the language, they managed to make friendships, just by smiling and doing their work sincerely, and in mainly nonverbal ways showing that they were just trying to be helpful. There was this one Tibetan who would eat in the cafeteria, where normally people would keep to themselves or sit in small groups. And one day he decided to buy lunch for a group of his co-workers. Before that, people would not ordinarily buy someone lunch unless they knew that person very well, but even though he did not know them well he bought them lunch. Then the next day, another person bought lunch for the group, to reciprocate. Then, others started doing that, and soon each day a different person would buy lunch, and through that they became closer friends."

I once heard the Dalai Lama remark that we can use our own lives as a kind of laboratory, where we can experiment with the implementation of the principles he speaks about, and investigate for ourselves the truth of his assertions. In thinking over his ideas about work and happiness during a recent trip to my local supermarket, I amused myself by viewing the shopping trip as if it was a controlled experiment designed by some clever researcher. The controlled experimental conditions: Take a half-dozen identical check-out stations, identical aisles with identical copies of the *National Enquirer,* identical cash registers, and identical racks of chewing gum and razor blades. The experimental variable: add the human factor—insert a different human being behind each cash register.

At this supermarket, there are two checkout clerks who have been working here for some years. I've ended up in each of their lines countless times. Jane is a woman in her mid-thirties. She goes about her job efficiently and quickly, yet she rarely says a word other than calling out for a price check. No matter when I've shopped there, she always seems to have a slightly sullen expression, almost on the verge of a scowl. Dorothy, on the other hand, a jolly lady in her late fifties, couldn't be more different. She always engages in friendly banter with the customers, is always smiling and helpful. She asks them about their lives and remembers what they say—she even remembers what they bought last time. It is a delight to listen to her. You can wait in her aisle, standing in line while the person in front of you unloads 137 items, pulls out a two-inch stack of coupons, and wants to pay with a third-party check, yet you don't seem to mind. Well, at least you mind less. Dorothy has a sincere interest in food as well as the customers, and often engages in a running commentary about the person's food choices, swapping recipes as she rings up purchases, "Oh, I haven't tried that brand of frozen pizza. Is it good?" "I see you bought Twinkies again—let me give you a tip—buy some of the Betty Crocker yellow cake mix, the kind with pudding in the mix, and slice up the pieces thin, then layer it with fresh whipped cream—it's like a homemade Twinkie, at least if your home happens to be in heaven!" (She was right!) She has always struck me as one who genuinely enjoys her work.

The difference between Dorothy and Jane not only illustrates the impact of attitude on job satisfaction, but also how one person can make a difference on those around her. Recently I was restocking a lot of food items at home, so my purchases filled two shopping carts. The bagboy offered to help push one of the carts out to my car, and we spoke as I was loading the groceries into my car. I've always noticed how Dorothy treats her baggers with respect, and some of the younger high-school students relate to her as a mother. As we were loading the groceries, the bagboy was telling me about how much more he enjoys his work on the days that Dorothy works, adding, ". . . and it's not just me. When Dorothy is working, everybody seems to be in a better mood, even the manager. I'm not sure why, but things just seem to go better on the days that she's working."

The prime importance of the human factor at work applies equally to any setting, a supermarket or the stock market, in a boardroom or in a boiler room. As the character played by Nicolas Cage in *The Family Man* exclaimed, "Whether it's on Main Street or on Wall Street, it's all just people!" So, no matter where we work, we've got to find a way to get along well with the people around us.

Some people work in a really tense environment, and may not be getting along with their co-workers. In those situations, do you have any thoughts on how to improve things?" I asked the Dalai Lama.

"This depends on the person, and their capacity and willingness to try to control their own emotions, like anger, jealousy, and so on. We should try our best to accept responsibility for our own emotions, practice tolerance, and try to reduce jealousy, although of course it isn't always easy and people will have varying degrees of success.

"But generally speaking, one could start by recognizing that we are all interdependent, we all depend on one another for our livelihood. That is the place we could start. The deeper our appreciation of that fact, that reality, the greater our willingness to work cooperatively with others will be. Sometimes we have a sort of feeling that we are separate from others, independent, the kind of feeling that *I earn my own money, I support myself, so who needs others?* Especially when we are young and healthy, there's that tendency to think *I can manage alone; I do not need to care about others.* But no matter what kind of job we have, there are many other co-workers who contribute in their own way to the running of the company that we depend on for our livelihood. Without them, the company simply would not exist, and we would not be able to earn our living, not to mention our customers, or suppliers, or many others who make it possible for us to earn our money."

"That's, of course, unless we work alone in our basement, having a job as a counterfeiter, printing up our own money," I joked.

The Dalai Lama chuckled politely at my meager sense of humor, then continued. "In fact, in the context of the workplace, which is what we are talking about here, in order to get along better with others I think the most important thing is to recognize our interconnection, our interdependence. That's the key factor. Have a clear understanding of that reality. At least on that basis one will be more willing to work cooperatively with others, whether or not one has any special feeling of affection or compassion toward them. On that level, on the level of building teamwork, compassion or empathy is not even required. However, if you want to enhance and strengthen the relationship, move it to a deeper and much more satisfying level, then empathy and compassion would be required. You understand?"

"Yes." I nodded.

"So, in thinking of other things that can help one deal with difficult people at work, I think that if one is in a situation where there may be hostile co-workers or demanding supervisors at work, a wider perspective can sometimes help—realizing that this person's behavior may have nothing to do with me, there may be other causes for their behavior, and not taking it too personally. Their hostile outbursts may actually have more to do with unrelated issues, maybe even problems at home. We sometimes tend to forget these simple truths.

"And also I should mention that if we are talking about trying to cultivate a deeper compassion for others, that compassion should be unbiased; ideally it should be directed toward everyone equally. That's genuine compassion, universal compassion. For example, often we think of compassion as something that is directed toward those who are worse off than you, less fortunate people who are poor or in some difficult circumstances. There, of course, compassion is a completely appropriate response. But often if someone is more wealthy than you are, or famous, or enjoying some fortunate circumstances, we feel that they are not appropriate objects for our compassion. Our compassion dries up, and we may feel jealousy instead. But if you look deeper, no matter how rich or famous someone is, they are still a human being just like you, subject to the changes of life, of old age, illness, loss, and so on. Even if it is not apparent on the surface, sooner or later they are subject to suffering. They are worthy of compassion on that basis, on the basis of being a fellow human being. So, this relates specifically to the workplace, where people are often in conflict with their supervisors, bosses, but one is more likely to feel envy, fear, or hostility rather than to think of them merely as another human being, as worthy of your compassion as anyone else.

"So, this brings me to the final approach to dealing with difficult people at work, these trying situations. And this depends entirely on the basic outlook, orientation, and personal interest of the individual. But in this regard, there are some people who have an interest in spirituality, those people who are trying to train their minds, to cultivate spiritual values like compassion, patience, tolerance, and forgiveness. Now, for those people, they may use these challenging situations as part of their spiritual practice, and view situations where there are conflicts with difficult co-workers as opportunities to practice these wonderful human qualities, to strengthen these spiritual values. I think it is a wonderful thing if one can use one's place of work as a place of spiritual practice as well.

"As I usually mention, however, practicing patience and tolerance does not mean that one should passively allow oneself or others to be harmed in any way—in those cases, one needs to take appropriate countermeasures. But this has to do with one's internal response and reaction to conflicts at work, or to situations that may cause emotions like anger, hatred, or jealousy to arise. And this approach is definitely possible. In my experience, for instance, I have met many Tibetans who have been imprisoned, political prisoners, by the Chinese for many years, being beaten, starved, tortured. And yet they were able to use their spiritual practices even in these extreme conditions, and in some cases even strengthen their spiritual practice while maintaining compassion even toward their captors.

"For example, there was one senior monk who was imprisoned by the Chinese for many years. A group of his students was also in the same prison. I once met a monk who was one of the students of this senior monk. He told me that all of them were mistreated and abused in this prison, but it was especially hard on the students when they saw their teacher being beaten and humiliated. They became very angry. But the teacher advised them not to be overcome by hatred, that this was in fact an opportunity for inner development. He spoke to them about the importance of maintaining their compassion, even toward their guards, who were sowing the seeds for their own future suffering by their misdeeds."

The Dalai Lama looked at his watch and realized it was time to close. As our meeting drew to an end, he suddenly started to laugh heartily. "Anyway," he remarked, "today I've been giving you suggestions about dealing with difficult people at work. Even though I'm talking about these things, if I went to work for a company and was in those kinds of adverse situations with employers or co-workers, I do not know how far I would be able to follow my own advice. I don't know—I might start stomping around, yelling and breaking things, throwing things through windows and breaking glass. I might get fired! And later on, if we make a book about these discussions, there's a danger that one of the readers might come to me and say something like, *I've been in this very difficult work situation, so since you have made such a wonderful presentation, be in my place for at least one week! Then you will be in trouble.* Anyway, thank you, Howard. Good night."

"Good night. Sleep well, and I'll see you tomorrow."

Chapter 3

MAKING MONEY

We met again the following afternoon, picking up where we had left off in our discussion about some of the most common sources of dissatisfaction at work. As we had discussed the previous day, there was no doubt that a poor social climate, one full of conflict and jealousy, can make work a nightmare. Yet according to a Gallup survey, Americans generally tend to be more satisfied with the social aspects of their job than they are with matters of recognition, how much they feel valued at work. And for many people, one's salary or pay is viewed as an objective measure of how much they are valued by their employer. But in today's society, one's pay level often represents much more than that. It not only reflects how much one is valued by the employer, but how much money a person makes can be intimately connected with how one values himself or herself. It can be linked with our own sense of self-worth.

As a retired senior vice president at a major brokerage house explained, "For thirty years I was a hotshot broker, at the top of the game. There were days when I could make millions of dollars for my clients, tens or hundreds of thousands for myself. In one year I could make three, four, five times the investors' money. But the problem was, of course, that there were other days when I could lose as much. So for thirty years I was bouncing up and down like a basketball—during the periods I was making money, when I was 'winning,' I was unbelievably high. I felt like I could do no wrong, and my clients who were getting rich all heaped praise on me, telling me what a genius I was. And of course I agreed, I deserved every bit of their praise, I felt like I was the smartest guy on the planet. And during those times I'd be impatient, judgmental, and intolerant of others. But then there were the other times, the down times when people were losing money, even going bust. During those periods I would often sink into severe depression, I felt ashamed, and sometimes I'd just stay home and get drunk. Which of course didn't help things. I felt like a total failure, an idiot, and I'd even be afraid to face my clients. It got to the point a couple of times where I even felt suicidal."

For most of us, the link between how much money we make and our self-esteem isn't as dramatic as it was for this broker. But it illustrates an important principle. If we choose an external marker as the measure of our inner worth, whether it is the amount of money we make, or others' opinion of us, or the success of some project we're involved in, sooner or later we're bound to be battered by life's inevitable changes. After all, money comes and goes, and thus is an unstable source of self-esteem, an unreliable foundation upon which to build our identity.

Despite this, no matter what kind of work a person does, according to social scientists, around one third of American workers still see financial rewards, rather than the nature of the work itself, as the primary purpose of work, as the most important aspect of their jobs. These people are particularly prone to intense resentment and dissatisfaction if they feel that they are unfairly compensated for their efforts.

Thus, in our discussion about work and jobs, there was no avoiding the issue of money, and I was curious to hear the Dalai Lama's thoughts on the subject.

"I'd like to turn to the topic of money," I began. "Of course, when we speak of money, that is a vast subject that can be approached from a variety of angles, but for the purposes of this discussion, since we're focusing on work, I'd like your general thoughts about money as the primary motivation for one's work."

"Yes. I believe that for many their attitude toward their job would be simply to make money," the Dalai Lama affirmed. "There is nothing wrong in this. Since to survive in a modern industrial society everyone needs to find their own way of making a living, this attitude toward work as primarily a source of one's livelihood is very realistic. Particularly if the individual has a family, especially young children, to support through his or her job, there is in fact a dimension to work that is noble. The problem is, however, when the motivation to make money becomes an end in itself. When this happens, we lose sight of the very purpose of making money, which is to provide ourselves with the means to accomplish something. Money by itself is only a piece of paper. It is the value that we as a society agree to give to it that makes it valuable. The paper itself is worth very little. Its real worth is the cost of the paper it is printed on. It may sound silly, but I think it is important sometimes to be reminded of this simple fact.

"The trouble with pursuing money just for the sake of money is that this makes us a victim of greed, never-ending greed. Then we are never satisfied. We become slaves of money. I have some friends, I think I have told you about some of them in the past, who run here and there, travel all over the world in quest of more and more money, so sometimes I tease them, calling them slaves of money. But they never stop to think about why they are doing this, other than to make more money. Now, if such a pursuit did succeed in giving them the happiness and sense of fulfillment they seek in life, then I suppose there would be some justification for this. This, however, is not the case. In fact, the real problem is that they are never content with anything. Unless you become one of the few richest people in the world, which, in any case, is extremely unlikely, there is always going to be someone who has much more money than you. And when you obtain something, then you want something else. If you make a million, you want ten million, and when you have ten, you want a hundred million. So unless we learn to say 'that's enough for me,' we can never be truly contented. This is like a game where the goalpost is constantly being shifted so that you never have a chance to win."

"That may be true," I said, "but some people pursue money

not for the money itself, or even the things it can buy, but for the power it gives. Their motivation is power."

The Dalai Lama shook his head. "I believe that genuine power results from the respect that people give you. Real power has to do with one's ability to influence the hearts and minds of others. Mahatma Gandhi had true power, for example, but it was not based on how much money he had. Power based on one's wealth is artificial, only on the surface, and is not lasting. They are respecting your money, not you, so if you lose your money, the power and respect vanishes. It's like the power based on someone holding a gun—as soon as they put down the gun, there is no respect or power given to the person."

Pressing my argument a bit further, I said, "If we are talking about various motives for making a lot of money, I think one of the motivations for people to make more money is this underlying belief that the richer they are, the more freedom they're going to have. They have freedom to travel where they want, they have freedom to do what they want, there's a sense of, *If I become a billionaire I'll have total freedom. I can go where I want, do what I want.*"

"Freedom is a broad topic," he reminded me, "and here we are speaking about it in a limited context. And in this limited context, yes, there is a degree of freedom. For example, freedom from the burdening worry about finding financial resources. Freedom from worrying about food, clothing, and shelter. So in that sense, there is an element of freedom. If an individual or family is really struggling and their main preoccupation is day-to-day survival, then there would be a tendency to believe that if their financial conditions improved, everything would be fine, because that's what they are mostly preoccupied with.

"So, people need a certain amount of money. Money can be useful—it can buy food, medicine, provide opportunities, and even buy a place to live or a few vacations. O.K. And if one has more than one needs, it can be used to help others. That is very good.

"And there is another reason money can make a difference. The foundation of what I consider to be basic human values is a sense of concern for others. If someone is economically deprived, desperately poor, then the practice of human values is difficult for them. It is sometimes hard to have consideration for others when you can barely survive. For example, it is important to protect the environment, but if someone is hungry, someone may cut down trees or do slate mining so that they can eat. They have to think about the immediate needs of the stomach before environmental concerns.

"But here we are talking about one's basic orientation, one's attitudes toward money. We are talking about cases where one doesn't think of money merely as a means to provide one's basic necessities, such as food or shelter. You mentioned thinking of money as a means of achieving freedom. But for many people it even goes beyond that. There's a kind of underlying assumption that money can solve all of our problems. And even among Tibetans, even among those who have been exposed to the idea of spirituality and Buddhadharma, sometimes there's a tendency to feel that if you go to the States and earn a lot of money, then everything will be fine. In fact, there is a modern Tibetan expression for money, which is *kunga dhondup*. Literally, it means 'that which makes everyone happy and accomplishes all wishes.' Clearly there is a danger when somebody makes such an assumption. Now in certain countries, this kind of attitude may be understandable from a historical perspective—particularly in those countries in which the society emerged from an economically deprived state. In those societies the whole focus was geared toward economic development. There was this idea that if economic development is successful, then many of the problems of society will be solved. But even when conditions improved, there was this leftover way of thinking. And I think this was a result of neglecting the development of inner values at the same time. Or, one could say this way of thinking is a consequence or a side effect of the inability to recognize the value of inner potentials or inner values such as compassion, tolerance, human affection."

The Dalai Lama continued, "But, Howard, since you are from America, I think you would know better than I do the attitudes in America. In American society among the affluent people you've met, is there a recognition that they are all very contented, or are they feeling that something is still lacking, something still missing, they need something else other than wealth? What is the thinking of the majority?"

"Once they become rich?"

"Yes."

"Well," I answered, "in my own case I've met a number of people with hundreds of millions of dollars, and at least one billionaire. And my impression is being that rich doesn't make that much difference to their overall day-to-day happiness. Still, I know individuals who really enjoy having lots of money. For instance, some of them buy art and they really get a lot of satisfaction from buying their art. But overall, I think that rich people who are happy are just the same as poor people who are happy: if they give to charity and if they have good friends and good family relations, they're happy; if they don't, they're not happy. It's that simple—at least that's my impression. But I think that the scientific evidence, the studies, research, and surveys conducted by social scientists, are more important than my individual impression based on the few very rich people I've met.

"In our past conversations that led to our first book, I think we briefly touched on the subject of money. In that book I quoted some studies that presented evidence that beyond a certain point, at least beyond the poverty level, or once we have our basic needs met, having more money doesn't bring greater happiness. That was a few years ago. Since then, there have been more studies done looking at the same issue, and at this point the evidence has continued to mount, definitively and conclusively proving that having lots of money doesn't bring more happiness, there is simply no association. For example, just last year *The New York Times* reported that real income has risen over sixteen percent during the past thirty years in America, but the percentage of Americans who describe themselves as 'very happy' has actually fallen from thirty-six percent to twenty-nine percent during the same time period."

The Dalai Lama nodded thoughtfully as I continued, "In fact, the other day I mentioned a survey conducted by the Conference Board that showed that satisfaction at work has been declining over the past few years. That same survey showed that the largest decline in satisfaction came from those with the highest income. Unfortunately, however, these kinds of scientific findings, and even the common folk wisdom that money can't buy happiness, hasn't seemed to really affect the views of society in general. There still seems to be that sense that we would be happier if we were rich.

"So this brings me to a question—how would you convince someone who is interested in nothing but money to begin to realize that money doesn't bring happiness, to appreciate the inner values that you talk about as being the true source of happiness?"

"For those who have simply no appreciation of the importance of inner values, and no preparedness to even be open to the idea, then it is very difficult to explain," he uttered quietly, almost as if speaking to himself.

"Still, what would you say to a person whose primary motivation in work was the pursuit of more money, even if they already had enough to live on?"

"First, I might present the scientific evidence that you are referring to, showing that great wealth doesn't automatically result in happiness. Of course, people must decide for themselves how much money they need; but if they were very affluent and asked my advice, I might explain how if people share wealth they will be happier—more friends, better reputation, positive legacy, even less regret when they die. They can say to themselves, *At least I used my money to help others.*"

The Dalai Lama thought for a while. "Another thing—I would suggest that they simply pause and reflect upon the whole process of wealth creation. If they equate money with happiness, then they become engaged in this continuous cycle of wealth creation, even after becoming wealthy. They keep chasing after this elusive dream. They expand their involvement. They go after more. The more wealthy they become, the more problems they become vulnerable to. That's inevitable. So, one really hasn't achieved the kind of happiness and freedom one is seeking. Just the opposite: One is now a slave to money, in even greater bondage than at the beginning. And if one has not examined the underlying assumptions about what money will genuinely supply, then I've noticed that no matter how much money they make, no matter how high their salary is, there is still a kind of nagging worry about not having enough money. This is because the more money they make, the more lavish and expensive their lifestyle becomes, and then of course their expenses increase accordingly.

"There can be two main approaches of trying to reduce that worry. The first is to make more money, but as I mentioned, it is questionable whether this will be effective. The second is to reduce one's expenses, to deliberately have more modest desires. I think that is best, more sensible. So it would be helpful to take just a moment to ask, 'What am I doing? Why am I doing this?' And then see whether all of this money is really necessary, whether the activities are really beneficial. That simple act of reflecting, the simple act of pausing to consider, to reason, can have an impact.

"So, I feel that the critical issue is to ask, 'What is my basic outlook on life?' If the basic outlook on life is directed outwardly, externally oriented, and your basic assumption is *Yes, happiness comes from outside,* by external means, through the creation of wealth, then you end up perpetuating this cycle. If your basic outlook on life is, *Yes, money is important, but there are also other factors equally or probably more important for one's sense of well-being,* then I think you will lead a happier life."

"So, do you really think that would be a convincing argument, enough to get a person to change their outlook?" I asked.

"Now that's hard to say," the Dalai Lama laughed. "Even the Buddha wasn't able to change everyone's mind."

It was time for our customary afternoon tea break, and while we were drinking tea, one of the Dalai Lama's staff entered to relay a message. While they were speaking, I had a chance to think more about what he had been saying. Like many others in our consumer-driven society, I rarely took any time to reflect on my underlying assumptions and beliefs about money and the happiness it will bring. But it didn't take in-depth analysis to recognize the validity of his views. I could easily think of many examples of how the endless pursuit of wealth served to add layer upon layer of complexity to one's life. Among my wealthier friends I could readily see the exponential rise in the complexity of their lives the richer they became.

One couple immediately came to mind. They were both highly paid professionals, and they were thrilled when their income level finally rose to the point where they could afford their dream vacation beach home. With great anticipation, they looked forward to sipping piña coladas on their deck while watching the sunset over the ocean. Their fervor cooled a bit, however, as they became bogged down in lengthy negotiations, endless paperwork, and mortgage forms. When the transactions were complete, then came extensive renovation, followed by the inevitable arguments with the contractor due to escalating costs and construction delays. Then, furnishing and decorating—far more costly than they had imagined. By now, their excitement had diminished considerably. Their enthusiasm was revived for a brief period when they were finally able to enjoy their getaway for a few weekends, but after the first heavy rains they discovered a major flaw in the home's foundation, causing serious water damage.

I had run into my friends not long before, and asked them how they were enjoying their beach house. "Well, it is a beautiful house, and we really enjoy it when we can get away. Unfortunately, we don't seem to be able to get away and enjoy it as much as we had hoped. And on top of that, the mortgage payments, the maintenance, the utilities and upkeep, all made it a bit of a drain on our resources, so we're ending up spending more time at the office to pay for it, and we can't seem to find the time to get up there as often as we would like."

Our break came to an end, and the Dalai Lama continued his line of thought. "So, in the final analysis, even in the case of someone who pursues money just for the sake of more money, there is still somewhere in the depth of his or her mind the belief that this is somehow going to make him or her happier. The ultimate motivation still is to promote one's greater happiness. If this is so, then allowing oneself to become a slave of money and greed is self-destructive, it is defeating their very purpose.

Instead of promoting greater happiness, it brings misery, the suffering of never-ending wants. In contrast, those who never lose sight of the purpose of money and have the ability to relate to money with a healthy perspective, even though such people may actually possess less money, will enjoy a greater sense of well-being with regard to wealth and money. So, ironically, they may be poorer in terms of actual material wealth but they are in reality richer, for they are able to understand the true worth of money, and are freed from the unrealistic expectations about what wealth will provide."

Still thinking about the opulent lifestyle of luxury cars and vacation homes of some of my acquaintances, I couldn't help but contrast that with the life of simplicity led by those who lived here in Dharamsala, particularly the community of Buddhist monks and nuns. Thinking about this, I asked, "In the past, you've mentioned the Buddhist concept of 'right livelihood,' a concept that I'd like you to talk more about later. But I'm wondering, is there also a particular Buddhist approach or attitude about money?" I asked.

"The Buddhist concept of right livelihood does not have any implications of making any kind of moral judgments upon an affluent lifestyle, or the amount of money one makes. Of course, if an individual is a monk or nun, there are certain restraints coming from the monastic vows, which proscribe the individual from leading a certain life of comfort or life of luxury. For example, strictly speaking, a monk is not supposed to own more than one extra set of robes. So there are certain strictures like that, but if the individual is not a monk and there are no strictures coming from the monastic codes, if someone has been very fortunate and has great material resources, from a Buddhist point of view this is seen as fruits of his or her positive karma in the past. So right livelihood has no immediate connotation of simplicity versus luxury.

"Among the followers of the Buddha, there were royal members of various kingdoms. I feel that the Buddhist stand on the issue of wealth really has more to do with the mental state of the individual who owns the wealth and who earns it. There is an emphasis on training one's mind so that you will have no sense of possessiveness or miserliness on your part, that you are able to fully transcend any sense of possessiveness. And as for the wealth itself, there are some scriptures where there is an explicit statement that for a *bodhisattva,*[3] so long as there is a clinging, then even to own or possess a single coin is sinful, is unethical. But if the bodhisattva is free of clinging, then even to own great material resources is not incompatible with the ideal. So this seems to suggest that it is really the state of mind and the means by which you create the wealth that seems to be more important.

"In thinking about the Buddhist texts, all the excellences of human existence—such as material affluence and so on—probably from the Buddhist point of view are not something to be discarded. Also in regards to this there is in one of Nagarjuna's texts a discussion of four legitimate human pursuits, two goals and their corresponding means of attainment. One goal is ma-

[3] A *bodhisattva* is a person who has cultivated the altruistic intention to become enlightened so that he or she may be better able to help all beings.

terial fulfillment, and the means for that is creation of wealth, which today would include the accumulation of the most powerful U.S. dollars. The second goal is the attainment of liberation, and the means for that is spiritual practice. So, this is the Buddhist view."

The Dalai Lama's position was clear. Our attitudes about money are more important than the amount we make. As always, in our pursuit of happiness, our inner resources assume a greater role than our material resources, unless of course we exist in abject poverty and are suffering from hunger or starvation.

We had spoken of those who are "slaves of money," those for whom pay or salary is the prime consideration in their work. While this is true of many, there are clear signs that this may be changing. In his book *Authentic Happiness,* Martin Seligman, PhD, one of the key figures in the study of human happiness and the field of positive psychology, states, "Our economy is rapidly changing from a money economy to a satisfaction economy." He asserts that personal satisfaction is rapidly gaining on financial rewards as the determining factor in many individuals' choice of work. He points out, for instance, that law is now the highest paid profession in America, yet for many, money alone is no longer enough to entice individuals to enter and continue the practice of law. In fact, the major New York law firms now spend more on keeping their staff than on recruitment, as many attorneys are abandoning the practice of law for other kinds of work that may not pay as much but which will make them happier.

I recently witnessed a surprising example of this kind of attitude shift. Last month I was in need of a new personal assistant, and I placed a small ad in my local newspaper. I was shocked when 165 people responded in the first two days. Many of the applicants were highly qualified, previously working in positions of great responsibility, high-paying positions, and some were older individuals with many years of work experience. This was not a high-paying position, and I wondered if this might be a reflection of the poor state of the economy and the lack of jobs. I began to question some of the applicants as to why they were considering this job that, in many cases, they were clearly overqualified for. In looking at some of their résumés, I was certain that they could get a higher-paying job. I was surprised by what I heard. Many of the applicants told me that they had turned down positions that would have paid much more, and the responses of many were almost exactly the same as one person who explained, "Money isn't the most important thing to me anymore. I'm more interested in a job that allows flexibility, variety, and time to do other things. I don't want to sit at a desk doing the same thing every day. It will give me the flexibility to pursue my writing and my art. Plus, I like helping people. In my last job, I was working morning and night and I made a lot of money, but I felt that ultimately my work went to make a bigger profit for the CEO, whom I never even met, and a lot of faceless unknown stockholders. I want a job like this one, working as someone's 'right hand,' which will let me see how I'm helping someone, and let me see their face."

Yes, things may be changing. More and more people seem to

be making decisions in the very same way that a friend of mine aptly described recently.

"When I graduated from Barnard College at Columbia University, it was 1986, the height of Wall Street mania and yuppie madness. I had done several internships at art galleries and performance art centers—it was clear I had an affinity there. I was an art history and music double major, and it was something I could do with my major besides teach. I loved art and theater, so what could be better? At the internship discussion group at Barnard, we were going around the room talking about job offers and helping each other decide which one to take. I told them about mine. One was a very low-paying entry-level job at one of New York's most prestigious performing arts centers. The other was a job doing public relations in a Wall Street firm. They were offering three times what the arts center was offering, with a chance to at least double my salary every year in bonuses. When I asked the group what I should do, I was met with a chorus: 'Take the money!' But I saw what that kind of job had done to my brother—one-hundred-hour work weeks, no vacations, no social life, sleeping at the office, walking around like a zombie. I opted for the entry-level job in the arts, and though I often had to dig spare change out of the couch to find enough money to take the subway on a cold and blustery day (I usually walked to work), I ended up in a career I love, and eventually made enough money to take cabs when I want to. And I even have time for vacations."

Chapter 4

STRIKING A BALANCE: BOREDOM AND CHALLENGE

"Work has been driving me crazy lately," complained a friend who works as a marketing consultant. "I've about had it! In fact, I'm thinking about quitting. I just can't stand it anymore."

"Yeah, I know what it's like," I commiserated. "Work overload can be really stressful."

"Naw, it's not that. It's just the opposite. I've been bored out of my skull . . . same damn thing every day. I'm usually finished with what I need to do by two o'clock, and I spend the rest of the day trying to appear busy, trying to balance my pencil on its point, making paperclip sculptures, or on a really bad day staring up at the little holes in the ceiling tiles and playing imaginary games of connect the dots."

Boredom and lack of challenge have long been identified as common sources of dissatisfaction at work. Numerous scientific studies and surveys, such as those conducted by Sheila Henderson working at Stanford University or Karen Loscocco and her colleagues, sociologists at SUNY Albany, have confirmed that challenge is one of the primary factors in job satisfaction. In fact, experts in the field of organizational environment and worker satisfaction often speak of the concept known as "person-environment fit." To enjoy maximum work satisfaction and performance, workers must find a balance between two poles—with too much challenge on one end and not enough challenge on the other. With too much challenge, workers experience stress, strain, and deterioration of work performance. With too little challenge, workers become bored, which equally inhibits job satisfaction and hinders performance.

In view of the prominent role of challenge or boredom in happiness at work, I raised the issue with the Dalai Lama, explaining, "You know, in talking to my friends as well as looking at the literature on worker satisfaction, it appears that boredom is quite a common source of dissatisfaction at work."

He nodded, commenting, "I think it's quite natural for human beings to become bored if they engage in a repetitive activity. At a certain point some kind of fatigue sets in, some kind of dislike or unwillingness or lack of enthusiasm in the activity."

"Does that happen to you as well?"

"Yes," he laughed. "For example, recently I did a two-week retreat, an intensive retreat on Avalokitesvara,[4] with the recita-

[4] Avalokitesvara is the Bodhisattva of Compassion, the patron deity of Tibet. The Dalai Lamas are considered to be living emanations of Avalokitesvara. The current Dalai Lama is the fourteenth in a succession that dates back six hundred years. The retreat often includes 1,000,000 recitations of the deity's mantra—in this case, *Om Mani Padme Hum.*

tion of the six-syllable mantra and as a completion, at the conclusion of the retreat, I had to do certain empowerment rituals for three days. They're very long, complex rituals, so on the third day when the end was approaching, all day I was thinking, 'Oh, I don't have to do this tomorrow!' I was looking forward to it being over. This is very natural for human beings."

"Personally, how do you deal with that?"

"In my own case, my overall attitude to life and work and my basic frame of mind perhaps exert a great influence. For example, every morning I reflect deeply upon a verse from the very great seventh-century Indian Buddhist master Shantideva. It begins, 'For as long as space remains . . .' Do you know that verse?"

"Yes." I nodded.

He continued reciting,

For as long as space remains,
For as long as sentient beings remain,
May I too remain
And dispel the miseries of the world.

"Personally, this verse has been a tremendous source of inspiration for me. I reflect also on other similar verses, such as the hymns to Green Tara composed by the First Dalai Lama Gendun Drup, which give me deep inspiration and reinforce my dedication to the ideal of altruism.

"I recite these verses and reflect upon them and make the aspiration that I'll dedicate my day as much as possible to being of service and benefit to others. Then I deliberately project the thought that I'll be able to spend my entire life in fulfilling this ideal. Thinking about the vastness of time, as referred to in Shantideva's prayer, 'as long as space remains . . .' really has a tremendous power in it. This idea of the vastness of time, and that kind of long-range dedication, makes a huge difference.

"Once in a while I confront situations where there might be a certain reluctance on my part, thinking, *Oh, I've got to do this, oh, what a chore*—for example, today I had to attend the proceedings of the exile Tibetan parliament, and initially there was this feeling of *Oh, I've got to do this, what a chore!*—but immediately I reminded myself this too is part of my service, this too is part of my work for the benefit of other sentient beings. The moment I make that connection, immediately that kind of reluctance and uninterest disappears.

"So, of course this is my way of dealing with these situations, but this may not apply to everyone."

Certainly on one level, the Dalai Lama's approach to dealing with boredom may not apply to everyone—after all, few of us have jobs as Buddhist monks or leaders of the Tibetan people. But just as certainly it would seem that the underlying principle could be applied to all of us—renewing enthusiasm and reawakening dedication by reflecting on the wider purpose of one's work.

As I was about to follow up on this, however, another thought occurred to me. His brief reference to his political duties reminded me of how actively engaged in the world he is. I thought about his many responsibilities, demanding duties, and how hard he works. It made me wonder even more how he could claim, even in jest, that he has no job—the words *I do noth-*

ing still echoed in my mind. Since he had mentioned some of his occupational activities, I hoped that this might be an opportunity to satisfy my curiosity about how he views his own job, and to discover how he remains happy despite the heavy burden of his responsibilities.

He had touched upon the subject of how he personally deals with boredom. For many of us, boredom arises when we are engaged in some kind of repetitive task and we are not adequately challenged. I decided to shift the focus slightly and approach the subject from a different angle, by soliciting his thoughts on the importance of challenge at work. Certainly he had faced his share of difficult and challenging work. He had cautioned me that his experiences as a monk or political leader may not apply to everyone, but I knew that he was involved in many other kinds of activities as well. I decided to select one of his more conventional activities—his role as a teacher—and use that as a way to introduce the subject of difficult and challenging work.

"I heard that you were just in South India, and the rumor is that you gave some very difficult teachings there, very complicated."

"Yes, that's true," he laughed. "In fact, I had to do a lot of homework ahead of time to prepare for those talks. At this teaching there were around nine thousand monks, and of course many of them are students who study these texts, so in their mind these subjects are very fresh. To me, they are not that fresh anymore."

"So it seems that you had to prepare a lot, and that it involved a lot of hard work?"

"Yes. Ever since I agreed to give the teachings, almost a year before, I had a little anxiety about it. So for two weeks before I went there, I read seriously and made notes for three hours every morning. The teachings were to be five hours each day for five days. So when the teachings began, on the first day I still had some anxiety, but after I started the first session, then I felt a little more comfortable. I felt, *Now it's O.K.* Then the second day, third day, fourth day, every day things got a bit better."

"I'm curious, did that hard work create a sense of satisfaction for you?" I asked.

"Yes, in fact, on the last day I felt tremendous satisfaction, tremendous relief. I'm finished! Of course, in this case the feeling of satisfaction was due, at least in part, simply to the relief of anxiety. But overall, it seems that the harder the work, the greater the sense of satisfaction. So, generally I feel that if you face this kind of hardship right now, later on it's definite that you will enjoy a special sort of satisfaction—happiness will come. So, hardship is the seed of happiness, the foundation."

"You're saying that you went through a lot of hardship and it contributed to a sense of satisfaction. I'm wondering then—do you feel that work needs to be challenging in order to be fulfilling? Is that an absolute requirement for satisfaction at work?"

"Probably it's better not to have the challenge," he replied.

"Huh?" I wasn't sure if I heard correctly. He had just got finished acknowledging the satisfaction one gets from accomplishing some challenging work. "But you just said . . ."

"Challenges are always there. Life will always present challenges," he explained. "They are always present in life; we are bound to encounter them. We don't need to add any additional problems. What we need to do is transform the challenges we do have into an opportunity—"

"What kind of opportunity?"

"Opportunity for creating greater happiness," he answered. "So when these challenges come, you should welcome them, embrace them willingly, and see them as a way to develop yourself, to prosper, to ultimately achieve a greater sense of well-being and happiness. Challenge can have this positive purpose, this benefit.

"I think for progress to take place, for further development, whether it is mental work or physical work, I think challenge is very necessary. For example, in Buddhist studies, debate is a very important tool for progress. We have to spend many hours going through the process of presenting our standpoint, having our views challenged and addressing and responding to these challenges. By engaging opposition, a deeper understanding of one's own standpoint emerges. If you just think about your own viewpoint and you have no willingness to open yourself to opposing viewpoints, there will be no room for growth or improvement. Welcoming challenge will help tremendously to sharpen your mind. Without it, the mind will go soft. Isn't it?"

I nodded in agreement. On this point there is general accord between East and West: both sides acknowledge the importance of challenge. In fact, as far back as 1776, the political economist and philosopher Adam Smith, a dominant figure in the development of Western capitalism, echoed the sentiments of the Dalai Lama. In his highly influential *The Wealth of Nations,* he wrote that a person who spends his life engaged in the same repetitive tasks tends to lose "the habit of exertion" and "generally becomes as stupid and ignorant as it is possible for a human creature to become."

Well, perhaps Mr. Smith was a bit more extreme than the

Dalai Lama in his views. But the Dalai Lama made clear his position on the matter of challenge:

"So whether we are talking about mental activity or physical activity, challenge can stimulate or promote development and creativity. In these challenging circumstances, your creative nature is fully engaged, fully utilized, whereas if you are in a situation where things are just routine, where there is no challenge, there is a danger of stagnation, there is no further development. Of course," he laughed, "if your life is being challenged, threatened, it's always better to run away. Those kinds of challenges are best to avoid rather than embrace. For example, if you are chased by a mad dog, it's not going to lead to much joy and satisfaction if you try to embrace that dog or that challenge—it's better to run away. And of course a mosquito or bedbug requires ruthless countermeasures, it's the only way!" His mischievous laughter trailed off as he added, "I should mention of course that when talking about the benefits of challenges on the job, this implies that there is a possibility to overcome the challenge, that the work or task is not so difficult that it is impossible to overcome."

"Well," I went on, "let's say you have a job where there are no challenges, some kind of very boring job where you just show up each day but it doesn't require your skills, your talents, your intelligence. There's no challenge there. Scientific research clearly shows that human beings tend to be more dissatisfied with their work in that kind of situation, without that element of challenge. So, when someone is confronted with work that doesn't challenge them, can you think of ways deal with it? Do you think it's a good or bad idea to create challenges to make it more satisfying?"

"I don't know." He laughed. "If a person has some kind of job on an assembly line, the same each day, fixed tasks that require little challenge, very boring and routine. . . . I don't know how to create challenges at that job unless you break something or sabotage the machines!

"But anyway, Howard, I think you need to recognize that among human beings there are many different dispositions and temperaments. Some people, particularly more intelligent people, tend to like intellectual challenges and problem-solving, but they may not like work that requires physical effort. Others may prefer less challenging work. For example, I met one Tibetan, a former monk, who likes to do very unchallenging work, the kind of routine physical labor, repetitive tasks that don't require a lot of thought. So during that work he likes to think about *Dharma*.[5] That work frees his mind to think about other things.

"Now, in saying that this monk prefers nonchallenging work, I think it's important to keep in mind that challenges come from

[5] The term *Dharma* has many connotations, but no precise English equivalent. It is most often used to refer to the teachings and doctrine of the Buddha, including the scriptural tradition as well as the way of life and spiritual realizations that result from the application of the teachings. Sometimes Buddhists use the word in a more general sense—to signify spiritual or religious practices in general, universal spiritual law, or the true nature of phenomena—and use the term *Buddhadharma* to refer more specifically to the principles and practices of the Buddhist path. The Sanskrit word *Dharma* is derived from the etymological root meaning "to hold," and in this context the word has a broader meaning: any behavior or understanding that serves "to hold one back" or protect one from experiencing suffering and its causes.

all sorts of areas of our life. For example, for a spiritual practitioner or one who seeks to cultivate universal compassion, responding to one's enemies with empathy and compassion can be seen as a challenge. Acting with kindness, and even showing affection toward one's enemies, now that's a great challenge! But if one can do that, and eventually even see some positive result, then there will be a tremendous sense of satisfaction and happiness. So, for those who seek to practice compassion, responding to the sufferings of the poor, the weak, the unprotected, and the helpless, these are challenges. Challenge doesn't necessarily mean something that is obstructive or negative. Nor is a task a challenge to a person if he or she doesn't care anything about the matter. For example, the suffering of the poor may not be a challenge for someone who simply does not care. However, for a practitioner of compassion, it certainly is. So, I think there will always be individual differences in what someone may or may not consider to be a challenge, as well as the level of challenge that they prefer.

"So," he concluded, "when you speak of work, I think it is important to keep in mind that there will always be so many different kinds of people, I don't think you can categorically say that challenging work is better or unchallenging work is better. I don't know. It just depends on the person." He paused, and began to chuckle. "Personally, I think no challenge is better because without challenge you can just lie down and rest. Take a little nap."

"Seriously, do you really think that if there is no challenge at all in one's work that one can still gain a sense of fulfillment and satisfaction from that work?" I asked.

"I don't think that challenge is an absolute requirement for satisfaction and fulfillment. For example, the natural expression of warmth and affection, relating to other people in that way, is effortless. It doesn't require a lot of challenge, but you do get a lot of satisfaction from that."

"That's true," I admitted.

Summarizing the latest findings of social scientists, Edwin Locke, Dean's Professor Emeritus of Leadership and Motivation at the University of Maryland, College Park, has said, "Research shows consistently that mental challenge—assuming one is willing to respond to the challenge—is a critical determinant of job satisfaction." Despite the clear-cut link between challenge and work satisfaction, Professor Locke suggests that one's willingness to respond to the challenge is also an important factor. This is where individual variation comes into play—as the Dalai Lama rightly points out, there may be individual differences in the degree of challenge that one requires, or is willing to meet. Some may thrive on highly challenging work, while others may be less willing to take on challenging work. So, as we seek to optimize our happiness at work, it is for each one of us to decide what level of challenge provides the greatest degree of growth and satisfaction.

As the Dalai Lama reminds us, relating to others with love and affection is a rich source of satisfaction that can seem effortless. In fact, life offers many such moments of satisfaction, moments which can arise spontaneously, effortlessly. This sense of deep fulfillment can occur while we are engaged in many different kinds of human activities, in virtually any setting—and of course the workplace is not completely devoid of such experiences.

Many years ago, one of my chemistry professors told me about an experience he had had while working in his lab. "I was in the middle of a difficult but interesting experiment as part of my research. After taking a morning coffee break, around ten-thirty, I set down my mug and resumed my work. After what seemed to be around five or ten minutes, some of my grad students came into the lab and started asking me some questions. I was right in the middle of making some notations, so I was reluctant to stop what I was doing, and I was a little annoyed that they were bothering me just as I was getting started, and I wasn't supposed to meet with them for many hours yet, at three-thirty. Anyway, I put down what I was working on and looked up at the clock. It was almost four o'clock. I had been working for over five hours, and yet it was as if no time had passed, and it was completely effortless. Not only wasn't I tired, but I was filled with energy. I didn't remember anything I had been doing during that period, and yet when I reviewed my notes, I had made tremendous progress on what was a very difficult problem. I had been completely absorbed in what I was doing. I couldn't believe it. That evening I had an enormous sense of accomplishment and a kind of energy that seemed to last for a couple of days."

Although this was many years before I first heard the term, the professor had perfectly described being in the state of "flow" while at work. The concept of flow was first introduced by psychologist and social scientist Mihaly Csikszentmihalyi (pronounced: *chick-SENT-me-hi*), and over the past three decades Dr.

Csikszentmihalyi has been investigating and refining this concept. The term "flow" describes a mental state that most of us have experienced at one time or another. To be in flow means to be totally absorbed in whatever one is doing at the moment. It occurs when one is fully present and completely focused on the task at hand. One can be in flow while playing basketball, sculpting, solving a difficult math problem, involved in a business transaction, rock climbing, or simply in a deep conversation with a friend or lover. Essentially, flow can occur during any human activity, whether at work or at play, whether it is primarily a physical, mental, or social activity.

While flow can occur under a variety of different circumstances, researchers have found that the specific characteristics of this state are quite uniform and stable: the same characteristic features of this state are present in any given activity or setting. There is also a particular set of conditions that are required to create this state. Flow arises when we are engaged in an activity that we feel is important, meaningful to us, and worth doing. Flow is more likely to occur when there are clear-cut goals to the activity, and we receive some kind of immediate feedback about our progress as the activity unfolds. The task must be challenging and require skills, but there must be just the proper balance between the challenge and our capabilities—people in flow feel that their skills are being fully engaged in the task at hand. And even though the project may be challenging and require skills—at that moment it feels effortless. While in flow, we find ourselves engaged in the activity for its own sake alone, not for any external rewards we might receive. The task is intrinsically rewarding, in and of itself.

"You know, one of the reasons I brought up the topic of challenge at work," I said to the Dalai Lama, "is because it relates to a concept that seems to come up frequently these days in the psychological literature, the concept of 'flow.' Challenge is one of the factors required to create this state of flow. This concept is increasingly mentioned in articles on human happiness, and this state can commonly occur at work. Are you familiar with the concept of flow?"

"No," answered the Dalai Lama. "Can you explain to me what you mean by that term?"

"Well, briefly, this concept involves a particular state of mind that occurs when our attention is completely focused on a particular task or project that we are doing at the moment. It is a state of intense concentration and deep involvement in the activity. While in flow, one loses a sense of time, it's as if time stops and a person is fully in the present moment, not thinking about the past or future. The person is so immersed in the activity that they even lose a sense of self or identity, the sense of self vanishes, there are no thoughts about 'me,' such as *I'm doing this*, or *I'm feeling that*.

"Anyway, while engaged in the activity, there's also a feeling of effortlessness, a sense of total control over what one is doing. Take, for example, a professional tennis player. They've practiced and practiced for many years to hone their skills, and now they are in a match with a difficult opponent. They get to a state where all of their skills and all of their learning and capabilities meet the challenge from the opponent and create a kind of balance. Their physical movements and high state of concentration all help to create the state of flow.

"Although flow can occur in any activity, some investigators have found that Americans experience more flow at work than they do in their leisure time. Some of these researchers feel that people experience more flow at work because that's where we are likely to encounter challenges or opportunities for problem-solving, the need to exercise our skills, and it's an environment that encourages us to focus on the task at hand.

"For example, let's say you are giving a talk to a large audience and the topic is very complex. The material is very difficult and challenging, yet you've prepared, you've studied, you've developed certain skills, abilities, and knowledge of your field. These conditions could give rise to a state of flow where you're so absorbed in the material that you're not even thinking about how your speech is going, you're not even thinking, *I'm the Dalai Lama.* You lose all track of time and self-identity."

The Dalai Lama listened attentively. "The kind of mental focus you are referring to where there is a total fusion with one's immediate activity sounds to me like a quality of mind referred to in Buddhist psychology as 'meditative stability.' I believe that each of us can develop the capacity to focus our attention on any chosen object or activity for a prolonged period of time. One of the characteristics of such a focused mind is its total absorption in the chosen activity. In some cases, even disturbances in the immediate environment have no effect in undermining the depth of concentration. I have known individuals who had achieved such states of mind. For example, Gen Nyima-la, one of my earlier teachers, had an amazing capacity for focus. Often when he would enter into deep contemplation, I could see his facial expressions undergo visible transformation. When he was in that state, he became almost oblivious to his immediate physical surroundings. For example, if a student came to pour him a cup of tea or something, he simply would not notice this. There was a kind of total fusion of his mind with his contemplation. So to me, that probably is what this 'flow' is that you are describing."

I interrupted here. "Yes, that sounds similar. So, when someone is engaged in work, and they are in the flow state, they get to a point where they are totally absorbed in the work purely for the sake of the work. They are so focused on it, they're not doing the work for money, they're not doing it for fame, they're not doing it to advance their career, they're not even doing it for the benefit of society. They're just so involved and concentrated on the work that the work itself becomes a source of satisfaction. So my question to you is, do you have any thoughts on how to create that state at work?"

"First, if you are seeking satisfaction from your work, I think that when a person is in that state of one-pointed mind, it's not possible to gain satisfaction at that moment, because satisfaction is a different kind of mental state than the state of total absorption that you are describing."

"You raise a really good point," I remarked with great interest. "In fact, the research has found the very same thing, noting that when someone is in that state of flow, you don't see them smiling and thinking about how happy they are or how much fun they are having. The sense of satisfaction comes later. So you're right. But my question still is, from your perspective, are there ways to create the conditions to be in that flow state at work, whatever one's work happens to be?"

◆

The Dalai Lama paused for several moments, then said, "The value of such a focused mind is recognized in many ancient spiritual traditions. In fact, in some of these traditions, such as Buddhism, we find practical methods for developing and enhancing a stable mind. So, I think that undertaking some practice of stabilizing meditation will probably help.[6] Because in stabilizing meditation you choose any object and try to focus mentally on it. Perhaps that might at least help focus one's mind, and familiarize the person with that kind of concentrated mental state."

The Dalai Lama continued, "Then of course there are other factors that could contribute to the likelihood of achieving that state. For example, you mentioned that the flow state arises when one is engaged in some challenging work or solving some problem, and one's skills and abilities are used to meet that challenge. So it is dependent on one's skills and knowledge of the task at hand. This suggests that one can increase this state by increasing one's familiarity with the particular work or subject. It can be a matter of constant study and familiarization, becoming habituated to a particular way of thinking or doing some task.

"And another factor can be involved—I think one would be more likely to move into that state of flow if one has a high level of interest in the subject or the kind of work to begin with. So, in the example of Gen Nyima-la, he also had great interest and familiarization with the subjects he was focusing on.

"But I also think that the state you are describing, that kind

[6] See Appendix, page 209, for the Dalai Lama's instructions on a basic stabilizing meditation.

of state where one loses a sense of time or even identity, can arise in different contexts or under various conditions. I don't think it is necessarily associated with happy or positive mental states. I think it can be associated with both happy states or unhappy states. For example, sometimes when you are totally gripped by fear and become paralyzed by the experience, you can experience a loss of time. When I am giving a series of teachings on a text, if I am enjoying the experience of teaching, I tend to lose any sense of time. On the other hand, if I come across points that are extremely difficult and I am struggling with my commentary, then the contrary experience occurs: Here I feel as if time is dragging at a very slow pace. So this phenomenon of loss or distortion of time can occur when one's mind is in a totally relaxed and joyful state, when one is fully concentrated and is delving deeply into a discursive analysis, as well as when one's mind is gripped by more negative emotions such as fear. When this experience occurs, one of the obvious signs is the total obliviousness to the events in the immediate physical surroundings."

He continued, "For example, there could be occasions where you're too scared, almost scared to death, then at that time also you remain totally absorbed and without any sensitivity. So, here one could be in a state where one loses a sense of identity, of time, of place, and so on, one is totally in the moment, but it is not voluntary. It is not due to interest or engagement in some interesting problem or work. It is because of fear, lots of fear, almost as if you are in shock.

"I'm wondering—when I fled from my home when the Communist Chinese invaded, I was so frightened that I might have experienced that 'flow' state for a moment." He laughed. "My mind was blank, in a state of thoughtlessness." His unrestrained laughter mounted as he recalled, "I also remember when I was seven years old, I was reciting a prayer I had memorized at a huge gathering, I think there were several thousand monks there. So, here were thousands of monks in front of me, and also high government officials. I was completely . . . I don't know if this is the correct word: confounded. I was totally in a state of no thought. I had memorized it so well, I had spent the previous few months practicing the recitation daily. So, once I started the prayer it went very fluidly, and because of the training it was automatic. But my mind went totally blank. After two or three minutes there was a break, and then I noticed some pigeons going here and there, and in front of me I saw the *umze,* the chanting master. And then I was fear-stricken. When I look back these days, I think that the fright that I experienced on that occasion may have even shortened my life."

"Well," I responded, "I don't think the kind of blanked-out state when one is in a state of extreme anxiety and the flow state are the same thing. Now, I have to confess that I'm definitely not an expert in the study of flow, but I would guess, for instance, that if they did a PET scan or EEG and measured the areas of activity in the brain during your recitation when you were in front of thousands of monks and experiencing extreme performance anxiety, and again under different circumstances when you were totally absorbed in some work that put you in the kind of state of flow that I'm talking about, it would be two different things, two different areas of the brain being activated. For one thing, when you are in flow, you can be very relaxed, it is a calm state . . ."

"You really like this 'flow,' Howard!" the Dalai Lama exclaimed with an amused chuckle.

"Well, I don't want to beat it to death, but it does seem to come up a lot these days, particularly when reading about the latest theories of happiness. And some of the literature seems to describe this state almost like a kind of peak human experience, one that encourages growth and the achievement of one's full human potential."

"The thing about theories," he mused, "is that they may enjoy some popularity for a while, and everybody talks about these things, but then they may get replaced, or at least refined, by another theory. But I understand the difference in what you are describing. So, if I am understanding correctly, this 'flow' denotes that time passes effortlessly for you. And also you are voluntarily undertaking something. And that it is something interesting, something that you would like to engage in and then you would get totally absorbed in it."

"That's right," I said.

"Then, as I mentioned, there may be some things, like certain kinds of one-pointed or also analytical meditations that may be helpful. But no matter how nice that state may be, I don't think it is the most important source of satisfaction, fulfillment, or happiness."

I thought back to the first time I heard my old chemistry professor describe that state of complete immersion in his work, that complete loss of identity and sense of time. Even now, it still sounded pretty damn good to me, I thought.

"Why do you say that?" I asked.

"Because, for one thing, you can't be in that state at all times.

Now, through our discussions and through the book that we are working on, we are trying to create another kind of 'flow.' One that can be maintained twenty-four hours a day. That is our main aim—to come up with something we can use even when we are passing through a difficult period, factors we can use to help our mind remain calm—happy, even—when things are not going right. That's what we are trying to do.

"So, through this 'flow,' even if you get some temporary kind of happiness it will not be an ongoing thing. What we really need is an ongoing source of satisfaction, of happiness. For example, when we talk about *tantric* practices of developing great bliss,[7] even those very high states of bliss and ecstasy can't be maintained twenty-four hours a day. So I think this flow state is not reliable or sustainable, and I think it's much more important to develop other sources of satisfaction through one's work that are brought about by training one's mind, shaping one's outlook and attitude, integrating basic human values in the workplace. For example, dealing with one's destructive emotions while at work, reducing anger, jealousy, greed, and so on, and practicing relating to others with kindness, compassion, tolerance; these are much more important and stable sources of satisfaction than simply trying to create 'flow' as much as possible."

[7] Tantra refers to a system of meditation practices that involves channeling highly refined states of mind and subtle bodily energies. It is said that when the practitioner becomes adept at these techniques and attains high states of realization as a result of these practices, they also experience profound levels of spiritual bliss.

. . .

Flow has been described as an optimal human experience, and certainly if one is seeking happiness at work it's easy to understand the attraction of entering into a state in which the work itself becomes intrinsically rewarding, associated with a deep sense of fulfillment and gratification. But the Dalai Lama raises a critical question: As a primary source of happiness and satisfaction at work, how reliable is the flow state?

The evening after our conversation about flow, I thought about what the Dalai Lama had said. I suddenly remembered a part of my professor's story that I had conveniently forgotten. After the professor finished describing his experience, I asked him if he had ever experienced that before. "Oh, yes," he replied, "that same kind of thing has happened to me at least a half-dozen times over the past couple of years." Clearly, as the Dalai Lama points out, the flow state leaves something to be desired as a primary source of happiness and satisfaction. According to a Gallup poll, around one fifth of American workers report experiencing some degree of flow on a daily basis, with flow defined here as being so completely absorbed in their work that they lose track of time. But more than one third indicated that they rarely or never experience it. These figures are not limited to American workers either, as a German national survey discovered the same ratios among German workers. Researchers have used a variety of methods to quantify the experience of flow in daily life. Whether using qualitative interviews after the experience, written tests, or "real-time" measures using a method called ESM (experience sampling method), there is no doubt that flow tends to occur intermittently, typically only for brief periods, and is not something an individual can deliberately sustain throughout the workday. As with most other human characteristics, there is considerable individual variation, with some people more prone and some less prone to experiencing flow.

When talking about human happiness, whether at work or at play, the Dalai Lama once reminded me that there are different levels and categories of happiness. In one conversation, which was recounted in our previous book, *The Art of Happiness,* he distinguished between two types of human satisfaction: pleasure and happiness. Pleasure can certainly provide a temporary kind of happiness and engender intense emotional states. He explained that pleasure arises on the basis of sensory experiences, but since it depends on external conditions, it is an unreliable source of happiness. He pointed out, "True happiness relates more to the mind and heart. Happiness that depends mainly on physical pleasure is unstable; one day it's there, the next day it may not be." To the Dalai Lama, true happiness is associated with a sense of meaning, and arises on the basis of deliberately cultivating certain attitudes and outlooks. One can achieve this type of happiness through a systematic training of the mind. The training involves rooting out destructive states of mind such as hatred, hostility, jealousy, or greed, and deliberately cultivating the opposing mental states of kindness, tolerance, contentment, and compassion. True happiness may take longer to generate, and requires some effort, but it is this lasting happiness that can sustain us even under the most trying conditions of everyday life.

◆

This brings us back to flow. In describing the type of satisfaction or happiness associated with the state of flow, most investigators make a similar distinction between pleasure and happiness, and place flow squarely in the second category. They view pleasure generally as the satisfaction of biological needs, and they distinguish the flow satisfaction by assigning a different label to that kind of happiness, calling it "gratification," "fulfillment," or "enjoyment." For these scientists, the value of flow goes beyond the intrinsic satisfaction of being in that state for a few minutes or a few hours. According to researchers Jeanne Nakamura and Mihaly Csikszentmihalyi, "Experiencing flow encourages a person to persist at and return to an activity because of the experiential rewards it promises, and thereby fosters the growth of skills over time." Thus, it is a force that moves us toward growth and achievement of our human potential.

But the Dalai Lama takes us one step beyond that. While acknowledging some value to the flow state, he feels that we do not need flow to motivate us toward growth—we can head straight toward the goalpost, and go directly after the happiness we seek. It begins by fully recognizing the supreme importance of the basic human values, which he feels are the source of genuine happiness, whether at work or at home—values like kindness, tolerance, compassion, honesty, forgiveness. Based on our complete conviction about the value of these human qualities, we can then set about training our minds, reshaping our attitudes and outlook.

Thinking again of my former professor in this light, it is easy to see that he wasn't exactly the poster boy for happy workers. While a brilliant scholar, prolific writer, and accomplished researcher, he was known for being cranky, impatient, overly demanding, and generally disliked. Many of his grad students dreaded working with him. Preferring to work alone in his lab, he had little interest in teaching, which he often left to his teaching assistants.

In the very same department, however, worked another professor whom I have thought of many times over the years. This man was certainly less accomplished than his colleague, and enjoyed little professional recognition. No matter what work he was engaged in, he was easily distracted—if a student popped in unannounced, he was always willing to stop what he was doing and have a chat. And more often than not, the discussion quickly turned from chemistry to baseball or the latest movies. There was no doubt that this man was unlikely to make any great new discoveries, and it is not unreasonable to guess that he had never once experienced the flow state. But he had a talent for teaching. He had a way of connecting with his students, inspiring many to take a genuine interest in chemistry, even though initially many found the subject both too difficult and too boring, a deadly combination. His grad students worshipped him, and he became a mentor to many of them, inspiring and influencing them well beyond the confines of the classroom. I could easily imagine the countless students who, over the course of his forty-year career, were inspired by his kindness, his willingness to help, and the genuine interest he took in the students' careers, even if they were just reluctantly taking chemistry as a prerequisite for another field of study. I am certain I'm not alone in remembering him fondly many years later. It is easy to guess which professor enjoyed a happier life, at work as well as at home.

• • •

I noticed the Dalai Lama's attendant and a few staff members loitering on the porch outside, and looked at my watch, realizing we were running past my allotted two hours. It seemed as if we had just started. I guess that in discussing flow, I had entered into a flow state. The Dalai Lama also seemed in no rush to finish. He paused for several moments as if fully absorbed in thought.

Finally, he spoke, adding another dimension to our discussion. "I think it is important as we talk about these things to keep the bigger picture in mind. Now we are focusing on a discussion of work and how it relates to happiness, and of course we can continue talking about how to be happier at work. But it is definitely possible that a person could have very routine work, work that might not be challenging and might even be boring, and yet they can still be happy people. The world is filled with examples of that. So in those cases, the individuals may have other sources of satisfaction and fulfillment, they would not be relying on work as a primary source of satisfaction.

"Take one example of a worker who has a very boring routine job, working every day from early morning to late at night. Now, if that person's sole source of satisfaction comes from the job, if they have no life outside of work, spending little time with family and friends, and if they do not even cultivate friendships at work, then I think there is potential for unhappiness there, and eventually even some mental problems. But if you take another worker who does the very same routine, boring job, but someone who has interests outside of work, spending time with their family, going out with their friends; they would be a happier person. They may not have interesting work, but they can still have an interesting life. So in that case, they may use their job simply as a means of making money, but derive their main satisfaction and fulfillment from other areas of life.

"So a happy life should have variety, be more whole and complete. One should not just concentrate on job or money. That's important."

No matter how much we enjoy our work, sooner or later we are bound to come upon periods when we feel less excited about our work, perhaps a bit bored, maybe just vaguely dissatisfied. Our work no longer supplies us with the sense of satisfaction and fulfillment that it once did. This can sometimes be a watershed in our career. For many, we may interpret this loss of enthusiasm as a signal, a sign that perhaps we chose the wrong career—maybe we're in the wrong field, and it's time to look for a new job, one that will awaken in us the joy and excitement that we once experienced. Of course, sometimes that is the case, but before turning to the classified ads, it may be judicious to stop and assess one's situation. As the Dalai Lama points out, experiencing periodic boredom at work is just human nature. It's normal. When his practices get a bit tedious, he doesn't give up his monk's robes, at least not yet. This is the principle of *adaptation* at work, an innate characteristic of human beings, a well-established feature of being human which has been thoroughly studied and documented by psychologists. So, no matter what life throws at us, good or bad, there is a tendency to get used to our circumstances.

In briefly referring back to this issue in a later conversation, the Dalai Lama noted, "People tend to get used to things, and sometimes may lose their enthusiasm. For example, in the first year that an individual got a job, it may have been a tremendously joyful event and the accomplishment may have given him or her a sense of fulfillment. But the very same work, if you happen to look at it in the second year, then it may give rise to a totally different response on the part of the individual."

The principle of adaptation suggests that no matter what kind of success or good fortune we experience, or, alternatively, no matter what adversity or tragedy we encounter, sooner or later we tend to adapt to the new conditions and eventually migrate back to our customary levels of day-to-day and moment-to-moment happiness. In one study at the University of Illinois, researchers found that within six months after either a misfortune or a happy event, subjects had returned to their usual state of happiness and no residual effects from the event could be found. Thus, you could be promoted to CEO unexpectedly with triple your salary, or you could suddenly experience the most devastating failure at work, yet less than a year later you'll find that you're about as happy as you were before.

Of course, there's a reason for this. From a Darwinian perspective, evolutionary psychologists argue that this characteristic has its roots in our remote past as a species. It was an adaptive feature that helped us survive. Thus, if someone was permanently happy from some success or accomplishment, in a perpetual state of bliss, that would tend to extinguish one's motivation for the continued development of new skills, for growth and progress. It would kill initiative. On the other hand, if people were naturally inclined to become permanently depressed or discouraged from a failure or loss, if months and years passed and it continued to hurt every bit as much as it had on the day it happened, again that would be disabling, and would reduce the odds that that individual would survive, pass down their genes, and become an ancestor.

This is why, as the Dalai Lama reminds us, we need a balanced life. No matter how satisfying our work is, it is a mistake to rely on work as our only source of satisfaction. Just as humans need a varied diet to supply a variety of needed vitamins and minerals to maintain health, so we need a varied diet of activities that can supply a sense of enjoyment and satisfaction. Recognizing that the principle of adaptation is normal, we can anticipate and prepare for it by intentionally cultivating a full menu of activities that we enjoy. Some experts suggest that one can start by making an inventory—taking a weekend to make a list of the things you enjoy doing, your talents and interests, even new things that you think you might enjoy if you tried them. It may be gardening, cooking, a sport, learning a new language, or volunteer work—any activity through which one can develop and exercise skills. So, if we go through a slow period at work, we can turn to our family, our friends, our hobbies, and other interests as our primary source of satisfaction. And if we shift our interest and attention to other activities for a while, eventually the cycle will swing again, and we can return to our work with renewed interest and enthusiasm.

Chapter 5

JOB, CAREER, AND CALLING

We met again the following day.

"You know, yesterday in discussing the link between work and happiness, you mentioned that sometimes we need to stand back and keep the bigger picture in mind. That reminded me that so far we have identified some of the more common sources of dissatisfaction at work, factors such as boredom, lack of autonomy, feeling that one is unfairly compensated, and so on. And you've also discussed some of the sources of satisfaction—factors such as human relationships or even potential sources such as challenge, which you mentioned depends on the individual. But in a broader sense, I'm wondering what you consider to be the most important factor. What factor plays the greatest role in influencing our happiness at work?"

The Dalai Lama remained silent. From his expression of deep concentration, I could see that he was carefully considering the question. Finally, he replied, "When we are talking about work, our goal, the most important thing, or goal, is a sense of fulfillment from one's work. Isn't it? So, in seeking to gain a sense of fulfillment from one's work, I think one's attitude is the most important thing. Yes . . . Attitude toward one's work is the most important factor." He paused again. "I think that, and also self-awareness, self-understanding," he added. "Those are the key things.

"But of course, as we discussed, there can be other factors as well. One's emotional make-up, the level of one's emotions such as jealousy, hostility, greed, and so on, can play an important role. For example, if someone gets a job and if the person has a sense of inner contentment and also is not greedy, then to that individual that work may be very fulfilling. On the other hand, there may be a second individual who has the same job but that individual may be much more ambitious and thinks that he deserves a better job than this and this work is too demeaning for him. He's jealous of other colleagues. Then the same work may not give a sense of fulfillment. So of course these kinds of factors make a difference."

There is ample scientific evidence in support of the Dalai Lama's claim that one's underlying attitude affects one's satisfaction and sense of fulfillment at work. Arguably the best research on attitude and general orientation toward work was a 1997 study conducted by Dr. Amy Wrzesniewski (pronounced: *rez-NES-kee*), an organizational psychologist and professor of business at New York University, and her colleagues, which showed that workers are generally divided into three distinct categories.

The first group views work as just a job. For them, the primary focus is on the financial rewards that the work brings. The nature of the work itself may hold little interest, pleasure, or fulfillment for them. Since their prime concern is the wage, if there is a decrease in pay or if a higher-paying job opens up, they are quick to drop the job and move on.

The second group of individuals views work as a career. Here, the primary focus is on advancement. Rather than financial motivation, these people are more motivated by prestige, social status, and the power that comes with titles and higher designations at work. In this category, there may be a much greater personal investment in the job, but as soon as the promotions stop, they start to become dissatisfied. Their interest in the job can evaporate, and they may even seek new work.

The final category is those who view their work as a calling. These individuals do the work for the sake of the work itself. There is less separation between their job and the other aspects of their life. People in this category tend to love their work, and if they could afford to, they would continue doing the work even if they didn't get paid. They see their work as meaningful, having a higher purpose, making a contribution to society or the world. As one might expect, those who view their work as a calling tend to have significantly higher work satisfaction, as well as overall life satisfaction, than those who view work as a job or career. Summarizing their findings, these scientists report, "Satisfaction with life and with work may be more dependent on how an employee sees his or her work than on income or occupational prestige."

Yet we don't need to rely on social scientists, occupational psychologists, or Harvard MBAs to prove that this is so. Each one of us can conduct our own investigation, using our own life and the lives of those around us as our research subjects. With a little reflection and observation, it is easy to discover how one's attitude can have profound effects on enjoyment and satisfaction at work.

Of course, our attitudes toward work can be shaped by many factors, both internal and external. Our childhood experiences, upbringing, and culture all may play a role. Like many others in our society, for instance, I remember my father speaking to my siblings and me about the virtues and pleasures of hard work, trying to instill in us the importance of a strong work ethic. And like many in our society, his nonverbal messages created an impression of work that was quite different from his words. Returning home exhausted every evening, and reluctant to talk about his workday, he created some uncertainty in our young minds about exactly what he did on the job. Judging by his demeanor, however, and not having much information to go on, we would not have been surprised if his work somehow involved sitting in a dentist chair getting a root canal from nine to five every day.

Based on this, I had no burning desire to enter the workforce. And as a teenager, my first day on a new job did nothing to revise my doubts about the virtues and pleasures of work. I had landed a summer job in a concentrated-orange-juice canning factory. My job involved standing at the end of a conveyor belt, removing boxes of cans and transferring them to a wooden pallet on a metal cart. The learning curve for my fascinating new job lasted approximately eleven seconds. By the end of the first hour, overcome by a mixture of tedium and exhaustion, I already started to resent the boxes as they relentlessly rolled down the ramp. I considered each box to be a personal affront. For the first five minutes, I amused myself by thinking about the classic *I Love Lucy* episode in which Lucy gets a job boxing chocolates off a conveyor belt, but I quickly discovered I was unlikely to encounter many wacky hijinks here. The plant seemed devoid of humor, and I was beginning to formulate a theory that the factory might be equipped with some kind of special industrial air filter, removing every molecule of fun. My co-worker standing across the conveyor belt seemed to lend some support to my unproven hypothesis. He was completely silent for the first hour on the job, and finally his first words to me were, "This job sucks!" He never told me his name. And to make things worse, he seemed to be deliberately slacking off. He moved so slowly that I was forced to remove and stack more than my share of the boxes. It was infuriating. Giving him the benefit of the doubt, however, maybe it wasn't just him that was moving slowly—time was moving so slowly at this new job that perhaps the laws of physics had ceased to exist inside this building. Each minute seemed like an hour, and all I could do was look helplessly at the clock. I didn't think I would make it past the first day.

On the second day, however, I received my very first lesson in the prime importance of attitude and how it can completely transform one's experience at work. There was a shift rotation, and my taciturn co-worker was replaced by Carl, an older man who was truly remarkable for his energy and enthusiasm. I couldn't help but marvel at the way he worked. He seemed to relish the physical movement, deftly removing the boxes with a rhythm and economy of motion that was a genuine pleasure to watch—like seeing a professional athlete engaged in a workout.

And it wasn't just the movement that he seemed to enjoy. He took delight in interacting with his co-workers. He knew everyone by name, full details of their personal histories, and he soon got me so engrossed in conversation that the day ended before I knew it. He genuinely liked people, and they liked him back. And he seemed to have an innate sense of the wider purpose of his job. At some point he had taken the trouble to find out how many cans of orange juice the factory produced, and to which states and countries the juice was shipped. He took pleasure in thinking about where the juice was going and would roar out farcical warnings, like "Careful with that box there boy, the o.j. in that box is goin' directly to Her Majesty's royal yacht, to be mixed with vodka and served up in highball glasses to bored diplomats," or, "Now, don't drop that, 'cause this orange juice is headed straight for Nebraska, where it's gonna be sucked out of a plastic bottle by a towheaded colicky little one-year-old." In thinking back to Carl, a man whom I have not thought of in almost thirty years, I came to see him as a classic example of a person who turns routine work into a calling.

Continuing with our discussion of attitudes toward work, the Dalai Lama offered an illustration. "When talking about one's attitude toward work, here's one example from my perspective as a monk. I've seen how attitude makes a big difference in how people go about doing their work and in the sense of fulfillment they get from it. I've noticed, for instance, how a young monk may enter a monastery and begin his religious and philosophical studies, and at the initial stages the monk may not have much of an appreciation of the deeper meaning of the texts, but he has to get up very early and stay up very late, and keep studying and doing chores. At this point, he feels this is a very tiring thing and he is very burdened, very bothered, and he would engage in it very reluctantly. He has no choice. Later on, however, he gradually starts knowing the meaning, starts appreciating the texts. He begins to see the deeper meaning and purpose of what he is doing, and this causes a change of attitude. Now not only will he do the job, but he will do it with great enthusiasm, and he doesn't show any sign of boredom or even physical tiredness. So even though he may be spending the same amount of time doing the same kind of thing, the change of attitude alone makes a big difference. And I think no matter what kind of work one does, attitude makes a difference."

"Now that we've established that attitude, one's view of one's work, is a critical component of satisfaction and happiness, I'd like to break this down a bit and go into more detail," I said.

The Dalai Lama nodded his assent.

"In terms of identifying attitudes toward work, there was a research study showing that generally speaking, in the West, people view their work in one of three categories: some people view their work simply as a job to earn money, where the wage is the primary interest and motivation; others view their work as a career, and the key point there is focus on career development, advancement, promotions, and going to higher levels in whatever their field is; and then the third category is people who view their work as a calling. The characteristics of a calling would be that they see their work as contributing to some greater good, associated with a sense of meaning. So, the concept of calling primarily has to do with the idea of a higher purpose of their work, maybe even the social good or welfare of others.

"Those are the three primary attitudes or views that people have of their work or job. About one third of people will see their work as a job, a third as a career, and a third as a calling. And further, the study showed that people who view their work as a calling are generally more satisfied and happier at work than those who see it merely as a job or even as a career. This certainly seems to support your idea that people's attitudes about their work can determine their sense of fulfillment."

"Yes, this makes sense," the Dalai Lama observed. "I would think that there is a greater potential for dissatisfaction at work if you are doing your job only for money, only to receive a paycheck and nothing else. And even with the view of work as a career, that could still potentially lead to dissatisfaction. Of course, it would depend on one's motivation, but if one was only concerned with career advancement, promotions, job titles and designations, there would be a danger of excessive competitiveness, frustration when you don't advance, and jealousy when others advance, and so on. That would not lead to an optimal state of work satisfaction. And there would be further danger of even making enemies. On the other hand, it is easy to see how viewing one's work as a calling would be more inwardly satisfying.

"And I think seeing your work as a calling might also have other positive effects. For example, earlier we talked about boredom, and you asked me how I deal with boredom, although I wasn't sure if my experiences could apply to everybody. But here, I think this is something that might apply to many people.

If you see your work as a calling, that would definitely help your mind not to tire easily. It would reduce boredom, and give you greater sense of purpose and resolve. And with that view, you could maintain your interest and enthusiasm even if you didn't get a pay raise or a promotion."

In exploring the three primary orientations toward work—job, career, and calling—we had spoken at length about the first category in our discussion about money as one's primary motivation for working. But the Dalai Lama was right in pointing out that a career orientation with the primary emphasis on promotion, job titles, and designations can potentially be equally a source of misery. Diane serves as an example of the potentially destructive consequences of career orientation associated with an excessive preoccupation with higher status and greater wealth.

Diane is a lawyer, a very talented prosecutor. Despite being an eloquent speaker, capable of swaying a tough jury with brilliant arguments and impassioned pleas, when asked why she became a lawyer she is suddenly at a complete loss for words. Perhaps this is because she has always been torn between two opposing views of her work: on one hand seeing her profession as a vehicle to wealth, status, and others' validation of her intelligence, and on the other hand seeing it as a means to protect people from criminals, from the predators who destroy lives and undermine society. Unfortunately, her "one hand" gradually became stronger than "the other" as her driving personal ambition overpowered her sincere desire to be of service to others.

She had started out in the attorney general's office with a

very promising career. She won case after case, rising up the ladder very quickly. But by her late thirties she couldn't resist the lure of the money being made by colleagues in large corporate firms, or in personal injury law. By the time she went into the private sector, however, she was facing a glass ceiling and age discrimination—she was too old to be a junior associate, and she had been in criminal law too long to make a lateral move. She became a solo practitioner but was never able to make the money or achieve the renown she so longed for.

Of course, that didn't extinguish her craving for wealth and recognition. In fact, it grew stronger over the years, fueled by her habit of pouring over alumni bulletins, professional journals, and local newspapers, furiously scanning the pages for reports of the latest achievements of her colleagues. Consumed by competitiveness and jealousy, each award or honor given to another attorney, each promotion to partner, each large jury award in a personal injury suit (of course calculating to the penny the 30 percent fee received by her colleague), was like a blow to her. The cumulative effect resulted in years of misery, and a growing bitterness which eventually eroded her relationships with friends and family.

Diane's steadfast refusal to let go of her endless quest for riches and fame in the private sector is particularly sad in view of her tremendous talent and abilities as a prosecutor. It has led her to continually turn down offers from the attorney general's office to return in a higher-ranking position and with much more visibility. Plagued by the accomplishments of her colleagues in the private sector, determined to match and surpass their success, she is virtually assured a life of continued unhappiness.

Commenting on Diane's chronic dissatisfaction, a former associate in the attorney general's office observed, "It's so sad, and so frustrating! Diane really has what it takes to be a great prosecutor, to really make a difference. And there are so many lawyers I know who would love to have her talent. I don't know, it's like she could never relax and enjoy her success, she always wanted something different. But the thing is, she's such an amazing prosecutor that listening to her complain about not getting what she wants in her private practice kind of reminds me of a beauty queen worrying over and whining about one pimple to a friend who has terminal acne."

Do you have any thoughts about how an ordinary person can change how he or she views work or attitudes toward work? In other words, how can we change our attitude from either the job or career approach to the calling approach? Are there any ways that you can suggest?"

The Dalai Lama thought awhile. "I'm not sure. But for example, let us imagine a farmer: when he does his work, how could he see it as a calling? Perhaps he could try to see the higher purpose to his work and then reflect on it. Maybe think about his taking care of nature, cultivating life. Or, in the case of a factory worker, he or she could think about the ultimate benefit of the particular machine they are making. I don't know. I think for some it might be difficult, but they can try to look for purpose.

"Now, I would think that certain professions, like social workers, teachers, health workers, would see their work as a calling."

"You know, interestingly enough," I pointed out, "you would

think that our view of our work depends on the nature of the job. In some jobs—for example, some kinds of unskilled labor, or what are considered menial jobs—you would think that people would see their job just as a means to earn money, while a social worker or a nurse or a doctor would see it more as a calling. But it is not the case that there is a division based on the job. In fact, the very same study that identified the three primary categories of how we view work found that there was the same division, no matter what the particular field or job. They studied a group of college administrators all with the same job, same level of education, same setting, and so on, and they found that a third saw their work as a job, a third as a career, and a third as a calling. So, even among nurses, physicians, or social workers, some just see it as a job, some see it as a career, focusing on more promotions or advancement, and some people see it as a calling. It seems to be based more on the psychology of the person and their view of their work, rather than the nature of the work itself."

"Yes, I can see how that may be true," said the Dalai Lama. "For example, the Buddhist monk students are supposed to study for a higher purpose—for liberation—but some may not carry that motivation. But that may be due to environment. Maybe they have no one who gives them good advice, helps them to see the wider view and the ultimate purpose. So if the social worker is properly trained and guided, and care and attention is paid to cultivating the proper motivation right from the beginning, then they might be better able to see their work as a calling."

"Well, obviously, if one is in a job like social work or other helping professions, there's at least a good potential there for that to be a 'calling' because they're directly helping other people, making society better. Now I'm just throwing around some ideas here, trying to clarify things, but I'm just wondering what your thoughts are about the achievement of excellence as the higher motivation or purpose of one's work—not necessarily helping society or helping others or a higher purpose in that sense, but a different kind of higher purpose: one is working because one wants to really achieve excellence in whatever activity they are doing. Such people want to develop their own personal potential to its highest degree through their work. So there the focus would be on gaining deep satisfaction purely from just doing a good job. Would you consider that to be a 'higher purpose' and put it in the category of a 'calling'?"

"I think probably that could also be categorized as 'calling,'" the Dalai Lama replied, but with a tentative inflection in his voice. "Now, generally speaking, personally I think it is best if the higher purpose or meaning in one's work involves being of some help to other people. But there are many different kinds of people, differing viewpoints, interests, and dispositions. So, I think it is definitely possible that for some people, the higher purpose may simply be striving for excellence in their work, and doing that with a sense of creativity. Here, the focus may be on the creative process, and the high quality of the work itself. And I think that could transform the view from a mere job or a career to a calling. But again, here one has to have the proper motivation—not carrying on one's work out of strong competition or a sense of jealousy. That's important.

"So, for example, I think in the past, and even now, there have been many scientists who are driven to carry out experiments just out of scientific curiosity and their strong interest in their particular field, just to see what they could find out. And I think these people could see their work as a calling. And as it turns out, often these scientists have made new discoveries, things which ultimately benefit others, even if that was not their original intention."

"I think that's a good example," I noted.

"Of course, there's a danger in that sometimes," he cautioned. "For example, there have been scientists engaged in research to produce new weapons of mass destruction. Particularly you Americans!" He laughed. "And I think they perhaps also saw their work as a calling, to come up with things to destroy the enemy, and perhaps in their mind to protect their own people. But then you have some leaders, like Hitler, who would use their discoveries in the wrong way."

I continued, "Well, as I mentioned, there are certain professions where potentially it may be easier to approach work with the 'calling' attitude. Fields like social work, medicine, religious teachers or high-school teachers. That type of thing. But we've mentioned the idea that there are millions of people who don't have the opportunity or interest to be great scientists or social workers, teachers or health care workers. Jobs where it is not as obvious how they have a higher purpose to benefit others, where it might be harder to view their work as a calling. For example, there are many jobs that are perceived as only interested in making money—bankers, stockbrokers, and so on—or interested in advancement, status, or power—corporate executives, lawyers, or other kinds of professions."

"Yes, that's true," the Dalai Lama replied, "but as I mentioned, there are many different people in the world, and so there may be many different approaches to discovering a higher purpose and meaning to one's work, which then leads to viewing one's job as this 'calling' that you are talking about. And then this would increase their work satisfaction. So, for example, a person may have a boring job, but that person may be supporting his or her family, children, or elderly parents. Then helping and supporting one's family could be that person's higher purpose, and when they get bored or dissatisfied with their work, they can deliberately reflect on providing for the happiness and comfort of their family, visualize each family member and how this work is providing food and shelter for that individual, and then I think this can give the worker more strength. So, then whether they like the work or not, there is still a purpose. But I think we have already mentioned that if you look at the work just for your own salary, no other purpose, then I think it becomes boring; you want other work."

"But of course there are still millions of single people who don't have a family to take care of," I pointed out. "Do you think there's a way of cultivating a higher motivation that they can remind themselves of in the work setting?"

"This is no problem," said the Dalai Lama without hesitation. "There are still many lines of reasoning a person can use to discover this higher purpose, the wider benefit of their work."

"Can you give some examples?"

The Dalai Lama pointed at the tape recorder on the coffee table in front of us.

"Now, look at this machine. I think at least a few thousand people had their hand in the making of this. And each one made a contribution, so we can now use this as part of making our book that might be of some help to other people. In the same way, there are many thousands of people who provide the food we eat, the clothes we wear. An individual worker on an assembly line somewhere may not directly see the benefit of his or her hard labor, but through a little analysis they can realize the indirect benefits to others and be proud of what they do, and have a sense of accomplishment. Workers all over the world are bringing happiness to others, even though they may not see this. I think that often if one works for a large company, on the surface it may appear that one's job is insignificant, that an individual worker doesn't have much impact directly on the big company. But if we investigate deeper, we may realize that our jobs can have indirect effects on people we may never even meet. I think that in a small way, perhaps through our work, we can make some contribution to others.

"Now, others, for instance, may be working for the government in some way, and thus see working for their country as the higher purpose. For example, in the 1950s there were many Chinese, including soldiers, who genuinely felt that they were working for the benefit of others, at least for the benefit of the Party, and that meant the benefit of the people. So they had a strong conviction of their purpose, and even sacrificed their lives. And they didn't care about personal gains. Similarly, in the monastic world there are many individual monks who choose to live in seclusion as hermits in the mountains, under basic conditions and great hardships. They have the option to remain in the monastery and have a life of greater comfort and ease. But because they have a much higher purpose in their mind, because their goal is to achieve liberation so that they can better be of service to all beings, they are willing to confront the immediate hardships. I think these people enjoy a certain mental satisfaction from their work."

The Dalai Lama sipped his tea as he reflected. "There is always a way to find a higher purpose to one's work. Of course, there may be some individuals who may not need to work because of their special financial circumstances. Under such circumstances, they can enjoy their freedom and enjoy the privilege they have, and that's one thing. But among those who need to work to make a living, then it is important for these individuals to recognize that, first of all, they are part of a society. They are members of the human society that they are living in. And also, they should recognize that by actively participating in this workforce, in some way they are acting out their role as a good citizen in their society, a productive member of society. And in this way, they can realize that indirectly they are making a contribution to the entire society. So if they think along these lines, then they can see some purpose in what they are doing that is beyond just providing a means of livelihood for themselves. That alone can be enough to give them a sense of purpose, a sense of calling. And this idea can be reinforced if they simply ask themselves, *What is the other alternative?* Just hanging around. Then there is the danger of drifting into some unhealthy habits, such as resorting to drugs, being part of a gang, or acting as a destructive member of society. So, there, not only are you not contributing to the society that you live in, but in fact you are undermining the very stability of the society that you are part of. If any worker thinks along those lines, they will see a higher purpose to their work."

The Dalai Lama paused again and laughed. "I'm thinking that

there may be a bit of irony here. We're discussing these things that may end up in a book, and it may seem that I'm making these suggestions to the American citizens, but whether the Tibetans, my own community, pay attention to these things is open to question. They don't always listen to me!"

"Well, maybe we can get our book translated into Tibetan," I kidded him.

Each of us has the capacity to cultivate greater work satisfaction—by transforming a job into a calling. And fortunately we don't need to chuck our job as a baggage handler or a mortgage broker and join the Peace Corps. No matter what kind of job we have, with some attention and effort we can find greater meaning in our work. Dr. Amy Wrzesniewski, a leading investigator in the study of worker satisfaction, has said, "Recent research has shown that people in menial jobs can transform their relations to their work and do so by shaping the tasks and relationships that are part of the job in ways that make the work more meaningful."

There can be many ways that a given individual can make work more meaningful. One woman, who works in a clerical position for a major corporation, described how she does this:

"Every day I pick out just one person who looks like they are having a peanut butter sandwich day, and I just make an effort to give them a word of encouragement, ask them if I can help in some way, or sometimes it's just giving them a smile and a pat on the back. Of course, that doesn't always help them—sometimes it does, sometimes it doesn't. But it sure helps me. It doesn't take much to do that, but believe me, it makes my day. It makes me look forward to going to work every day."

"What's a peanut butter sandwich day?" I asked.

"That's the kind of day where you wake up and right from the time you get up, nothing seems to go right. All morning, it's one thing after another, and then finally at lunch you drop your open-faced peanut butter sandwich on the floor—face down."

Of course, finding a greater purpose or meaning in one's work, adopting a different attitude or perspective, isn't always easy. The global impact of our efforts isn't always readily apparent. So, we must start on a smaller scale by acknowledging the positive effect we have on those in our immediate surroundings. And once we discover how we are contributing to the greater good, we must consistently remind ourselves of this, particularly when we become bored, overwhelmed, or demoralized at work.

Without the assistance of social scientists or organizational psychologists or experts like Dr. Wrzesniewski, a friend of mine who works as a senior editor at a large publishing house happened to stumble upon her own personal strategy to shift her attitude at work—a method she has been using effectively for many years, which perfectly illustrates how each one of us might go about turning work into a calling.

"With work, I often get to the point of feeling that I just can't take it anymore," she explained. "Who knows what the 'it' is, but every task feels like an unbearable burden, every question an insidious interruption, every meeting an imposition on my quality of life. In those moments, I can't help feeling I'd rather be anywhere but at work. I'd even rather be stuck on a hot, steamy subway, in a tunnel with no air-conditioning. Now, if I'm only focusing on my job as a career—as something to make me look better, or make me feel better—then this is the inevitable result. I've found that relying on something external for happiness will always let you down. My job can't make me feel better, I have to take care of that. So when I'm feeling like that, I don't try to do a wholesale shift in attitude—telling myself, 'O.K., my job ultimately results in people being helped.' That doesn't work. I have to start small. I have to start with the irritation I feel when I have to answer a nagging question from a co-worker. I have to appreciate that person as someone who also has a job to do and whose needs are at least as important, if not more so, than my own. Then I can take some satisfaction in the fact that because of my job I've been able to help clear someone else's confusion. From there, I can turn to the task at hand of, say, writing a marketing memo to position a book. Then I can think about how people in-house are reacting to that book—that it was comforting to them to read, that it was perfect for a loved one who was in the hospital and could they have another copy to send to their father? Then I think about the thousands of copies that will be in bookstores around the world and the people who might go in and buy the book, read it, feel helped, and pass the book along to someone else who might feel helped, and so on. So then I can see the purpose of my job is really to help alleviate suffering. But it's not easy to maintain. I slip into 'burnout' all the time. It's a mind-training exercise that I have to engage in all the time. And crabbiness at work is the sign that I need to do it again, and again, and again, until one day the feeling just comes naturally, spontaneously, and for a moment, while editing, I feel great joy that just comes out of nowhere."

Chapter 6

SELF-UNDERSTANDING

The Dalai Lama had been tied up in other meetings and commitments for several days, so when we resumed our discussion I was eager to pick up where we had left off. "The other day we spoke of how our attitude is a key factor in shaping our satisfaction at work, and we discussed ways that we might shift our attitude or outlook to view our work as a calling. But you also mentioned another key factor—self-awareness or self-understanding."

"That's right," said the Dalai Lama brightly.

Unlike most of our meetings, which took place in the late afternoon, on that day we began with a morning session. While not a "morning person" myself, I always enjoyed meeting with him at these earlier hours, as he always seemed so alert, refreshed, and in particularly good spirits. This morning was no exception, and he appeared to be as eager to resume our conversations as I.

"Can you explain in greater depth, then, specifically how this self-understanding might apply to our work?"

"Oh, yes. I think it can be very helpful if a person has better self-understanding. For example, if someone has very high qualifications and ends up with a bad job, then he has valid grounds to really complain and try to seek better employment. That's legitimate. He has the skills to advance, and he should advance. Whereas, you can have another person who also feels discontented with the employment he has, and wants a better job and more money, but that person's capacity and qualifications may not be very good. So here he has an inflated image of himself, he does not have accurate self-understanding. Instead of changing his attitude, becoming content with the work he has by realizing it corresponds to the level of his skills, he starts blaming others, demanding a better job, and his work becomes nothing but a source of dissatisfaction rather than a source of fulfillment."

"It's interesting that you brought up this issue of self-awareness," I commented, "because in reading the literature on the sources of satisfaction at work—why some people are happy, why some people are not—I find that some of the researchers talk about the same thing you mentioned: self-understanding and self-awareness as a key principle to achieving more satisfaction at work. Can you expand a bit on what you mean by self-awareness or self-understanding, more than just, 'Oh, I have the skills to do this job,' but in a broader sense—what would self-awareness and self-understanding include?"

The Dalai Lama elaborated, "Now, when we talk about self-awareness or self-understanding, there can be many levels. In Buddhist psychology, there is great emphasis placed on the importance of having a sense of self that is grounded in reality. This is because there is an intimate connection between how we see ourselves and how we tend to relate to others and the world. Needless to say, how we see ourselves also affects how we tend to react to a given situation. Now, on a very basic level, human beings have an innate sense of self, a sense of 'I,' that we perceive to be a kind of fixed, unchanging inner core, something that is independent, separate from others and the world. The question becomes, however, whether this sense of self, this 'I' that we cling to so strongly, truly exists in the way that we perceive it to exist. What is the true underlying nature of the self? What is the ultimate basis of the self? That becomes a critical issue in Buddhist thought, because we assert that this belief in a unitary, solid, unchanging 'I' is at the root of all of our mental and emotional afflictions, the destructive mental states that obstruct our happiness. Using reason, logic, and careful analysis, in searching for the ultimate nature of the self, we find that there is a gap between how we appear to exist and how we truly exist. A gap between appearance and reality. But this kind of investigation into the ultimate nature of the self, the nature of reality, is a matter of Buddhist theory and practice. It has to do with what is referred to in Buddhist language as *emptiness* or *no-self*. This is a separate issue from the kind of self-understanding that we are discussing here. Here, we are concerned primarily with self-understanding in the conventional sense. So we are not talking about arriving at the understanding of the ultimate nature of our self."

"Well, let's say that someone wants to develop greater self-understanding or self-awareness on this conventional, day-to-day level. How does one begin to do that?" I asked.

"Now, if you are talking about one's work or job," the Dalai Lama suggested, "if people wish to have a greater understanding about the level of their knowledge or technical skills in their particular field or profession, then they may want to voluntarily take certain tests that may help them find that out. I think that would help increase one's understanding of what one's capabilities are, at least on the level of technical skills, proficiency, or the type of knowledge that can be objectively measured.

"But if we are talking about increasing self-awareness and understanding on a deeper level, then the main thing is to have a view of self that is grounded in reality. Here, the goal is to have an undistorted view of oneself, an accurate appraisal of one's abilities and characteristics."

I considered this for a moment. Once again, I was struck by how the Dalai Lama's views, an amalgam of Buddhist wisdom and common sense, so closely parallel the findings of Western science. "You know, what you're saying reminds me of some of the recent theories advanced by certain researchers and experts in the science of human happiness. One researcher in particular, Martin Seligman, talks about increasing self-understanding by identifying what he calls one's 'signature strengths'—one's natural good qualities and characteristics, the unique set of virtuous traits that each one of us possesses. In fact, he and his colleagues developed a questionnaire or test that people can fill out to help them identify their signature strengths. He got quite sophisticated and detailed in compiling this questionnaire. He identified six main categories of human virtue, such as wisdom, courage, and love. He then subdivided these primary virtues into twenty-four 'signature strengths.' For example, Courage is subdivided into Valor, Perseverance, and Integrity. Anyway, this investigator maintains that one can become happier at work by identifying one's signature strengths and making a conscious effort to use these strengths on the job—every day if possible. He recommends choosing work where you can naturally use these strengths. But if you can't do that, then he suggests recrafting your present job to use these strengths as much as possible."

I continued, "Earlier, we talked about how people are happier at work if they view their work as a calling. We spoke about how one way to do that was by reshaping one's attitude and trying to discover a higher purpose or meaning to one's work. According to Seligman, there's another way to transform work into a calling—by identifying and using one's signature strengths. So in a way, I think this relates to the idea of self-understanding that you are talking about. At least on a conventional level.

"Talking about using one's signature strengths at work, I think you may be a good example of that. I remember that we've spoken in the past about your role as leader of the Tibetan people, and the degree of success that you've had. And in some of our discussions, you've mentioned, for instance, the differences in leadership style between you and the Thirteenth Dalai Lama. For example, the Thirteenth Dalai Lama was more austere, even severe. Your style, while different, might better serve the current needs of the Tibetan people under today's conditions. And you identified different traits—one being a kind of informality, another is a kind of straightforwardness, that type of thing. You identified what your strengths are and how they could be applied to the needs of your job, which is leader of the Tibetan people—at least that's one of your jobs. So that goes along with this idea of accurately knowing what your strengths are and then using them in your work. Does that make sense?"

"I don't know. . . . I'm wondering whether those would be called a style or a strength—my knowledge of English is sometimes limited. But I thought things like straightforwardness, informality, would simply be characteristics. I don't know if you could call them strengths. But what you seem to be saying is that if one's characteristics fit well with the circumstances, and can be useful, then that becomes a strength?"

"I guess you could put it that way."

"Because to me, things like honesty, truthfulness, humility would be strengths. So I'm not sure if I understand your definition. For example, I have a strong voice, a loud voice. That is one of my characteristics." He laughed. "And I give some lectures. So that is a strength?"

"Well, I don't think a loud voice would automatically be considered a strength, unless you're giving a talk and there are no microphones," I joked.

"That's very true, that's for sure," he concurred, his voice still ringing with amusement. "My brother recently went on vacation and stayed in a place where people with loud voices in the next room kept him up all night." His laughter escalated as he reminisced. "And I used to have one driver who sneezed so loudly that you could hear him from the other side of the building. So, explain to me more about this idea of strengths. What would be considered strengths?"

"Well, to be honest, I don't remember all the characteristics on Seligman's particular list; but, for instance, a loud voice isn't necessarily a strength, but the ability to communicate clearly and effectively might be considered a strength. Or, another example," I noted, as he was still shaking with mirth remembering the sneezing driver, "I've noticed that you've always had a great sense of humor, and have used that humor effectively to connect with others in many different circumstances. I think that would be a strength."

"But there," he said, "that just seems like a natural thing, a quality that just comes out. It just flows naturally. I don't consciously decide to use humor. So, I'm getting confused about this idea of strengths."

"Well, we're talking about self-understanding. And here, we are talking about identifying our natural positive qualities and abilities, and then using and applying those abilities in one's work. And in fact, once we identify our signature strengths, we can even try to enhance them, to build them up. In that way, a person can turn a job into a calling. It makes work more fulfilling, more satisfying. For example, the other day we mentioned that the teaching you gave in South India was hard work. I'm wondering if you used certain characteristics or certain abilities in giving those talks, and by using those abilities the experience was more fulfilling."

"I see," he said. "Yes, in that regard, I think I have one special ability—the way my mind works. I think I have a good ability to read a Buddhist text, and to get the gist of what is in the book and summarize it well. I think this is partly due to the ability to put the material into a wider context, and mainly my tendency to relate the material to my own life, to make a connection with myself and my personal experience, my emotions. Even in very philosophical texts and very academic topics, even philosophical concepts like emptiness, when I read books I make a connection with my own experiences. I don't separate my life into academic pursuits and personal experiences—they are interrelated. So then instead of the material or presentation becoming dry and academic, it becomes something living, something alive. It becomes something personal, something related to my own inner experience. Is this the type of thing you mean?"

It suddenly became clear why he was having trouble with the concept we were talking about. We had been discussing the idea of identifying one's personal strengths and then deliberately using them at work as a means of building greater satisfaction, of transforming one's job into a calling—but it seemed that his personal life was already so fully integrated with his work life that there was absolutely no separation between them. Thus, he had no need to try to come up with strategies to make him happier at work—after all, he claimed, "I do nothing" for a living, he didn't view any of his intensive activities in the world as work; these activities were simply an extension of himself as a human being.

Realizing this, I said, "Yes. That seems like a strength," no longer needing to pursue the point.

• • •

Toby serves as an example of how identifying and utilizing one's personal strengths at work can turn a job into a calling, how with some creativity and effort we can bring our strengths to work, increasing our job satisfaction. Toby is a recent college graduate who was delighted when he received his degree in accounting and went to work for one of the large accounting firms. He felt a sense of accomplishment that he had never experienced before, and was thrilled to discover the benefits of making a decent salary after his years of struggling as a student, trying to get by on minimum-wage, part-time jobs. But that initial elation soon wore off, and within six months he was reporting, "I started to get a little bored with my job. But I just couldn't put my finger on why exactly I wasn't enjoying it as much. The work was the same, my boss was the same, but for some reason I started feeling a kind of vague dissatisfaction with my job. Overall I still liked it, however, and I didn't want to change the kind of work I did. Anyway, I thought that I should do something outside of work, just to be less bored. I felt that I'd like to do something creative, because I have a creative side that I wasn't able to use at work. . . ."

"Yes," I injected, "creative accounting is what got Enron and WorldCom in trouble."

Toby chuckled and continued. "Anyway, I decided to take a night class in Photoshop, a computer graphics program. I loved it. So, after I finished the class, I was working on preparing a report at work, and I decided to include some fancy color graphs and other graphics in my report. It really looked great and I had a lot of fun doing it. One of my co-workers happened to see my report and asked me to do the same thing for a report she was doing. She showed it around, and soon others were coming to me asking me to punch up their reports. Finally, my boss noticed some of these reports and called me into his office. I thought that I might be in trouble because I was spending my time doing this kind of thing, and it wasn't number-crunching, which is what I was supposed to be doing. But instead he told me how much he liked these reports, that it really improved the quality of the presentations, and he changed my job description to include doing these computer graphics. I'm still working with numbers, which I also enjoy doing, but the new duties broke things up a bit and made work much more fun. I started looking forward to going to work again."

We've been talking about the importance of self-understanding," I continued, "and how one can increase self-understanding by increasing awareness of one's personal qualities, strengths, and so on. But you also mentioned something about self-understanding on a deeper level—having an accurate picture of who you are. Can you explain what you mean by that?"

"Yes," the Dalai Lama answered, "as I mentioned, it is important to have a sense of self that is grounded in reality, an undistorted recognition of one's abilities and characteristics. This is very important because a realistic sense of self has less potential for leading to psychological and emotional affliction. So first, I think it is important to identify the factors that obstruct greater self-understanding and awareness. One main factor perhaps is human foolishness"—he laughed—"simple stubbornness. By this I am referring to a kind of foolish stubbornness one adopts often in relation to one's experience in life."

"What kind of stubbornness?"

"For example, insisting that one is always right, feeling that the way you look at things is the best way to look at things, or the only way to look at things. This kind of attitude may sometimes provide a sense of protection, when in actual fact it closes the door to any real awareness of one's own possible shortcomings. Excessive pride, which often leads to an inflated sense of self-importance, will also obstruct the possibilities for greater self-understanding. For example, when you are arrogant, you are less likely to be open to other people's suggestions and criticisms, which are crucial for developing greater self-understanding. Furthermore, an inflated sense of self leads one to have unrealistic expectations of oneself, which has the consequence of putting excessive pressure on oneself. When these expectations are not fulfilled, which often is the case, this then becomes a source of perpetual dissatisfaction."

I asked, "So how does one overcome that kind of exaggerated sense of one's abilities?"

"The first requirement is that people actually want to overcome this. So here they could spend time thinking about the ways that this has caused them problems and suffering. Understanding the damaging effects of arrogance will increase their willingness to overcome it. Then, the next step would be simply to spend time reflecting on the many areas that they know nothing about, thinking about the things and knowledge they are lacking, looking at others who are more accomplished.

They might even think about the different kinds of human problems that all of us are subject to, no matter who we are. This may help reduce the level of arrogance and conceit.

"At the same time, an excessively low opinion of one's own abilities is also an obstacle. Humility is a good quality, but there can be too much humility. This kind of low self-esteem will have the negative effect of shutting out any possibility for self-improvement, almost by default, because the tendency of such a person would be to automatically react to an event with the thought, *No, I cannot do this.* So there, to overcome that, one should spend time thinking about one's potential simply as a human being, realizing that all of us have this wonderful human intelligence at our disposal, which we can use to accomplish many things. Of course, there are some people who are mentally retarded and may not be able to use their intelligence in the same way, but that is a different matter.

"In addition, I would also list an agitated state of mind as another obstacle for greater self-understanding. Since self-understanding demands a certain ability to focus on one's own abilities and personal character, a constantly agitated mind simply will not have the space to enter into any serious self-reflection."

"So, in those cases, do you think that practicing relaxation techniques, or certain kinds of absorptive or analytical meditations that you've spoken about, would be helpful? Assuming, of course," I had to add as a physician, "that there was not a medical condition that was causing the agitation."

"There's no doubt," he said decisively. "Anyway, to have greater self-awareness or understanding means to have a better grasp of reality. Now, the opposite of reality is to project onto yourself qualities that are not there, ascribe to yourself characteristics in contrast to what is actually the case. For example, when you have a distorted view of yourself, such as through excessive pride or arrogance, because of these states of mind, you have an exaggerated sense of your qualities and personal abilities. Your view of your own abilities goes far beyond your actual abilities. On the other hand, when you have low self-esteem, then you underestimate your actual qualities and abilities. You belittle yourself, you put yourself down. This leads to a complete loss of faith in yourself. So excess—both in terms of exaggeration and devaluation—are equally destructive. It is by addressing these obstacles and by constantly examining your personal character, qualities, and abilities, that you can learn to have greater self-understanding. This is the way to become more self-aware."

He paused, then added, "But what I am suggesting here is actually not something new, is it?"

"New in terms of what?"

"It seems to me that all these things are common sense. If someone just uses common sense, then all these answers will come."

"That may be true," I admitted, "but sometimes it seems that there is a general lack of common sense in our society. People can always use more common sense."

"I'm not sure that's true," he said, "because I think that common sense is required for progress, to accomplish things. You can't accomplish great things without some common sense. And I think in America they have accomplished many great things. So I think there must be some common sense there."

"Well, I guess you're right on that score. But still, people don't always take the time to stop and simply reflect, remind themselves of these commonsense things. And also, one can hear the same thing, the same common sense, and if your mother or an annoying uncle said it, a person would tend to ignore it, but if the same words came from you, people might pay attention."

The Dalai Lama laughed heartily. "Because I'm 'The Dalai Lama'? You know, Howard, we've just been talking about exaggeration, and now here I think you're exaggerating!

"Anyway, I think that self-appraisal—developing an accurate and realistic sense of self through careful observation—leads to greater self-understanding. And I think self-understanding is a crucial factor if one is talking about work satisfaction. It can even have other kinds of beneficial side effects."

"Like what?" I asked.

"For instance," he said, "would you say that one of the problems people experience at work is feeling bad and reacting very negatively when they are criticized by others? Or if not direct criticism, then at least relying too much on others' praise for their sense of satisfaction or worth, and becoming discouraged if they don't receive enough recognition?"

"Definitely."

This was a characteristic of workers all over the world. In fact, one study conducted by International Survey Research found that two of the top three priorities for U.K. workers involved receiving recognition for their job performance and being treated with respect.

"Now of course," the Dalai Lama continued, "having self-understanding, a realistic view of one's abilities, may not affect the degree to which you are criticized, but it can affect how an individual might react to that criticism. That is because this realistic view gives one a certain sense of self-confidence, a certain inner strength. They know what they are truly capable of, and also what their limitations are. And so they are less affected by what other people say. So if they are criticized, and it is valid criticism, they can accept this more easily and use it as an opportunity to learn something about themselves. Whereas, if they are falsely accused, they do not react so strongly because deep inside they know that it is not true, they know themselves. And if individuals are confident in recognizing their own positive inner qualities and their skills and knowledge, they don't need to rely so heavily on others' praise to supply that feeling of accomplishment."

The Dalai Lama ended by explaining, "If you recognize the tremendous value of self-understanding, then even if you try a certain kind of work or new job and you fail, it reduces your disappointment because you can look at that experience as a means of increasing self-understanding, as a way of knowing better what your capabilities or skills are or are not—you could look at it almost as if you were paying money to take one of those self-assessment examinations. And of course, self-understanding will reduce the likelihood of failure in the first place because you will not be undertaking things out of ignorance, taking on certain kinds of work that are beyond your capability. So, the closer you are to reality, the less disappointment and frustration you will experience. It will disappear."

The Dalai Lama rightly points out the importance of self-awareness as a key factor in happiness at work. His concept of self-awareness, however, goes beyond merely knowing what one's particular skills or talents are. To him, self-understanding requires the elements of honesty and courage in addition to self-examination—it involves coming to an accurate assessment of who one is, to see reality clearly, without exaggeration or distortion.

The benefits of accurate self-appraisal are clear. In a 2002 study led by Barry Goldman, PhD, JD, professor of management and policy at the University of Arizona, people with a strong sense of their own identity not only had greater work satisfaction, but also higher levels of personal well-being and overall life satisfaction. The study by Goldman and his colleagues defined personal identity as "a psychological state reflecting self-knowledge and a firm consistent sense of personal values and of one's ability to sustain one's conclusions in the face of opposition from others." Thus, greater self-knowledge was associated with confidence in one's own judgment, which suggests that one may be less affected by others' unwarranted criticism and may rely less on others' praise to supply a sense of self-worth. Further, researchers have found that in addition to having greater work and life satisfaction, those with a strong sense of identity may even enjoy other benefits, such as having fewer marital disputes.

◆

While the beneficial effects of self-understanding may be clear, the destructive effects of a distorted self-concept are equally clear. The negative outcome of a distorted self-concept can be amply demonstrated simply by examining our lives and the lives of those around us. In my own case, for instance, these destructive effects have been made readily apparent not only in my past professional life as a psychotherapist, but also in my personal life among my friends and acquaintances. Low self-esteem and underestimating one's abilities can be paralyzing, stifling personal initiative and inhibiting the individual from exploring new opportunities. Ultimately, it can obstruct the realization of one's full potential, preventing the achievement of one's goals.

Inflated self-image can be equally devastating, as the individual is constantly at odds with a world that refuses to see them as they see themselves—at the center of the universe, an unappreciated genius in a world of morons. In many ways, however, low self-esteem is easier to overcome than inflated self-image. Those with low self-esteem suffer from a tendency to blame themselves for everything, so at least they often recognize that they have a problem that needs to be addressed. They are much more likely to seek professional help to overcome their low self-esteem or associated disorders like depression, which are sometimes also present. Those on the opposite end of the spectrum, however, those with an exaggerated sense of their accomplishments and talents, tend to blame the world for their problems. After all, they are perfect, so it must be others who are at fault. They often fail to recognize how their arrogance and sense of entitlement drives others away, and may wonder why they have few close friends. While their actual achievements may be modest, when they fail to get the immediate recognition they feel they so justly deserve, they are quick to drop a project and fail to pursue their goals.

Once one recognizes the destructive nature of arrogance, how can one distinguish between that and healthy self-confidence? In one conversation that led to our first book, *The Art of Happiness: A Handbook for Living,* I once asked the Dalai Lama how individuals could tell if they were being arrogant or merely self-confident. He replied that those with self-confidence have a valid basis for their confidence, they have the skills and abilities to back it up; whereas arrogant people are not grounded in reality—they have no valid basis for their inflated opinion of themselves. I reminded the Dalai Lama that this would not be a helpful distinction for arrogant people, since they always feel they have a valid basis for their opinion of themselves. Acknowledging the difficulty in distinguishing between confidence and arrogance, the Dalai Lama finally shrugged his shoulders, laughed, and joked, "Maybe the person should go to the court to find out if it is a case of arrogance or confidence!" Moments later, however, he settled down and observed that sometimes one could determine this only in retrospect, by looking at the results of one's actions, whether they ultimately resulted in benefit or harm to oneself or others.

The first step in overcoming arrogance and inflated self-image is recognizing how damaging they are, and for that sometimes we need to analyze the outcome or results of our attitudes and actions. This retrospective approach may do nothing to change the results of our past mistakes, but it can certainly motivate us to reevaluate our attitudes, move toward a more accurate understanding of ourselves, build greater self-knowledge, and thus shape our future in a positive direction.

Fred serves as an illustration of the damaging effects of inflated self-image. I met him sometime back, following a talk I gave to a local writers' group. After my talk, Fred, a lanky, well-groomed man in his mid-forties, cornered me as I was leaving, asking for my advice. With a kind of professorial air and superior manner, he introduced himself as a friend of a friend of mine. He began by reciting his academic credentials, which were fairly impressive. He apparently had showed academic promise as a brilliant young student, graduating with a 4.0 average from a prestigious university at the age of nineteen. While up to this point in his life he had failed to fully live up to his early potential, he was quick to point out that he felt he was capable of great literary achievements. Explaining to me that he had a wonderful idea for a book based on some research he had done in graduate school, he abruptly and unceremoniously pulled out a large stack of loose papers from his briefcase, stating that this was a portion of the material he was planning on including in his book.

Within minutes he had asked me not only to read and critique his writing but also asked if there was anything I could do to help him find an agent or publisher. I explained that I certainly wished him well but that my schedule was too busy right then to agree to his request. Besides, I went on, there were a lot of people out there, English professors or professional editors, who were much more qualified than I to critique his writing.

Undaunted, he continued to press me, and since he was a friend of a friend of mine I reluctantly agreed to sit down with him for an hour or so and offer what advice I could.

We walked outside to a bench, and I began by reading the first twenty pages off the top of his stack to get a feel for his work. *This stuff is pretty good,* I thought as I paged through his material, but even to my untrained eye it seemed far from ready to submit to a publisher. I then explained to him in depth the process of getting a book published, giving him precise instructions on how to write a formal book proposal, the first step. I also gave him the names of a couple of agents I knew and a short list of some good books about how to get published.

I finished by offering words of encouragement, but stressing the importance of persistence—the key to success, in my view. I described how in my own case, *The Art of Happiness* was rejected by dozens of agents and publishers over a period of several years, and expressed how difficult it was for a first-time author to get published. After close to two hours, I finally excused myself, cheerily calling, "So, don't give up!" with a jaunty wave as I made my escape.

But it didn't end there. Over the next several weeks, having gotten my home phone number from my friend under some pretext, he called me several times at inconvenient hours, engaging me in long conversations about his ideas for the book. Finally, after four or five of these discussions, I spoke up, letting him know that while I certainly wished him the best, I had too many other commitments at the moment to be able to spend any more time helping him with his book project. And once again I repeated my earlier advice, giving him even more explicit instructions on the protocol for writing a formal book proposal, the procedure for finding an agent, and several additional books on the topic. I didn't hear from him after that.

Several months later, I ran into my friend whom Fred knew. I asked about Fred and how his book was coming along. My friend quickly apologized, saying that she has known him for years, but more than once he had embarrassed her by using her name as an introduction to someone, then promptly proceeded to ask that person for some kind of personal favor, as if it were owed him. She warned me that he would no doubt use my name as a means of introduction to the agents I had mentioned to him. She then reported that she had recently seen him, and gave me an update. He apparently had put his project "on hold." He had indeed called the agents I mentioned, as well as one or two others. In each case, he was able to get through to the agent using people's names, and as expected, each of the agents requested that he send a formal book proposal. To date, Fred had not done so.

Surprised, I asked my friend why he hadn't pursued this, knowing that even getting an agent to look at a proposal is an accomplishment in today's competitive publishing industry. She then told me how Fred felt that the agents should have been much more excited about his idea, and should have been able to decide whether they were interested in representing him or not based on his description of the book over the phone. Further, she said, Fred had mentioned that writing a book, or even writing a formal book proposal, would involve a lot of time and effort. He was unwilling to spend that time and effort purely on speculation—he felt that he should have a signed contract and some big advance money before devoting any more of his time to the project.

Needless to say, Fred is a classic example of how an exaggerated sense of our talents, abilities, and skills can sabotage our efforts to achieve our goals. But whether we are obstructed from achieving our goals by overestimating or underestimating our abilities and skills, there is little doubt that the greater our self-understanding and self-awareness, the more our self-concept corresponds with reality, the happier we will be at work or at home.

Chapter 7

WORK AND IDENTITY

There are few things in life that are as devastating to an individual as losing one's job. In what may be the most extensive study ever conducted on life satisfaction, in a survey of 169,776 people in sixteen nations, political scientist Ronald Inglehart found that unemployment was one of only a few factors that caused a significant decrease in life satisfaction.

"There's clear evidence that unemployment is linked with unhappiness," I began with the Dalai Lama one afternoon. "This is a significant problem all over the world, and I'm wondering if you have given any thought to that issue."

"You know, it wasn't until I became more familiar with Western societies that I first heard about how unemployment has such immediate impact upon families and individuals. And when I heard about this, I was slightly surprised because I had never even heard of it before. In the Tibetan language, we don't even have a word for unemployment."

"Why is that?" I asked with some surprise.

"Well, for example, here when we speak about employment or jobs, we are generally talking about the common nine-to-five type of job you see so often in Western countries. That concept was completely foreign to traditional Tibetan society. Of course, I'm not talking about the many modern Tibetans who live in the West or in urban settings. But in traditional Tibetan society, people were mostly farmers, animal herders, or merchants. The idea of set hours of work simply did not exist. In the West, economic conditions and societal structures are such that this kind of employment is an integral part of the concept of work.

"Among Tibetans, at least traditionally, the economic conditions are such that this nine-to-five daily employment isn't really an important part of it. In Tibet, either you are a farmer or a nomad or you are a merchant. The work is seasonal. Since this pattern is what they are accustomed to, it is seen as natural. So, if you look at the people living here in McLeod Ganj,[8] a lot of them now own shops, and many of them do a traditional kind of seasonal merchant business in Indian towns. During the season, they work very hard, and when they finish they come back and don't have any employment. In fact, I once suggested that while they are here in the off-season, we set up some kind of employment program, like cleaning wool or cotton or some kind of

[8] McLeod Ganj is a mountainside village in the area of the Indian town Dharamsala. McLeod Ganj is home to a large Tibetan community in exile.

employment. But they don't relate to this idea of unemployment, so my suggestion had little impact."

He rubbed his chin absently in thought. "Of course, in modern society, and particularly in industrialized nations, this issue of unemployment is a very difficult situation." He sighed. "There are no easy answers. I don't know. One has no choice but to try to cope, and make one's best effort to find new work. There is just no other solution.

"However, here again the basic attitude of the individual plays a very significant role, and can make a big difference in how someone responds. While we may not have control over our situation, our attitude is something that we have some control over. So first, what we need to realize is that uncertainty and change are very much a part of the modern economy, particularly with regard to employment. That is a serious problem, but a fact that we have to accept. There is no guarantee that there will be a job tomorrow if you are working today. So, if we understand this ahead of time, this may change how we respond when that happens. Then we won't feel so surprised, as if we are singled out. We understand that the loss of a job has many factors, the result of many causes and conditions. We will understand that, in many cases, it may even have roots in global economic issues. This way, we won't become so upset by taking it personally, or looking around us for someone to blame for our problems. This alone may help reduce our mental agitation. Of course, here we are talking about unemployment due to some wider causes or layoffs, not due to being fired because of one's own incompetence.

"So there might be different ways in which individuals will

respond to the challenges of change. What is important is to acknowledge this fact and try to work out how best to cope with the immediate problem itself. For example, if you need employment as a means of your livelihood and if you become unemployed, then all your efforts should be put into looking for new employment so that your livelihood will be secure. But there are two different responses. One person may feel demoralized and become sort of paralyzed, thinking, *There is no hope, I lost my job, what am I supposed to do?* But another individual in the same situation might look at it as an opportunity to make some changes. As a challenge. So that is the more positive way, a more proactive way of dealing with this problem. But of course it is not easy.

"There may also be other ways that might help at least reduce the mental anxiety of dealing with the situation, so that a person can use all their mental energy to find new work. For Buddhists, there are certain thought processes and considerations that help—for example, the belief in karma and ultimately taking responsibility for one's own karma. Although this kind of mental attitude may not have any effect in physically resolving the situation, at least it will help ease the individual from the psychological effect of losing the job, and so on. And of course, believers in other religious systems can also take some consolation in their own beliefs.

"As an aside, I should mention that when talking about concepts like karma, if they are not properly understood it could be potentially dangerous. Because in some cases people with only a partial understanding of karma can become very fatalistic. Their understanding of karma is that whatever happens is bound to happen anyway, as if the individual has no particular say, no particular role in the course of his or her life. But that is the wrong understanding. And if one has that kind of fatalistic interpretation of karma, then these religious concepts can become truly what the Communist Chinese say: religion is an instrument for exploiters, because the exploiters can say, 'What you are suffering at the moment is what you deserve, this is in your karma.'"

The Dalai Lama was right in pointing out the potential danger of misunderstanding the concept of karma, I thought. Among Westerners, I've often noticed the phenomenon he described: the inclination to blame the individual for his or her own misfortunes, or to view karma as simple fate, associated with a sense of resignation and hopelessness. If you lost your job, it's your own fault—you must have done something really bad in a past life; or, *I lost my job, but there's really nothing I can do about it—it's just my karma.*

These misconceptions are often due to the fact that the notion of karma is based on the law of cause and effect, the theory that one's current circumstances are the result of one's past actions, either in this life or a previous life. But what many of these individuals fail to take into account is the active component of karma. In fact, the root of the Sanskrit word *karma* means "action." And just as one's past actions may have contributed to one's current circumstances, one's present actions can change one's future. In addition, the Buddhist concept of karma is much more sophisticated than is commonly recognized in the West. For example, one's current experiences are the result of a complex interplay of past physical, verbal, and mental "actions." Through nonvirtuous deeds in the past, one may have laid the groundwork for negative consequences, planted the seed for future misfortune. However, through virtuous deeds and pure motivation, one may also ameliorate the manifestation of those consequences.

So, after a word of caution against misinterpreting the concept of karma, the Dalai Lama quickly returned to the issue at hand. "There is one other important issue to recognize when dealing with this kind of problem and one's reaction to losing one's job, or even to retiring. This has to do with one's self-image. Some people identify so strongly with their role at work, their self-concept is so mixed with the role they play or sometimes the amount of money they make, that it is as if they don't exist once they lose their job. Those are people whose value system places the greatest emphasis on money or status or those kinds of things, rather than inner values, basic good human qualities. So, for example, I've known some Indian and Tibetan officials over the years and have had an opportunity to observe how they respond differently to job loss and in particular to retirement. Among these officials, some have had their self-identity based primarily on their position, and would take a kind of refuge in their title. In many cases, these officials would bully their subordinates and generally revel in their power and position, or misuse their power.

On the other hand, I've known other officials who seem to base their self-identity more on basic human qualities and characteristics, identifying with just being a good person, an honest person, a humble person, and they would treat their subordinates accordingly. Then, I've seen what happens when their job is no more. Often the first category of individuals does not do well in that situation. They are abandoned by those whom they mistreated, and once they no longer have that job, it is almost as if their physical size shrinks, they have no sense of self, no sense of worthiness. But the others make the transition well. They are still respected by others as well as by themselves, they still have self-confidence—and in the case of those who retire, they look on it as an opportunity to explore new things. They respond to that situation with greater enthusiasm. They want to try things they have always thought about doing but never had the time. So, different people seem to respond to the same circumstances and situations very differently."

"I know exactly what you mean," I said. "When I used to practice individual psychotherapy, I encountered patients who lost their jobs, or who retired, and it could lead to severe clinical depression. I've seen powerful CEOs who lost their jobs, and if their identity was based primarily on work, it was like they became a living ghost. So," I asked, "if you were going to advise people, what would you tell them, what would be your advice to those who very strongly identify with the job that they have?"

"I'd advise them that they were incredibly foolish and stupid!" He laughed. "There's not much else to say, unless people are really willing to change their basic attitude. But the wise way to avoid, perhaps not the problem of job loss, but at least the mental agitation that may go with it, in this case, is to widen one's self-image, see oneself first as a human being with the capacity for friendships, for kindness, and so on, and then realize that one has different roles in addition to the role at work—one may be a parent or a child or a brother or sister, one may have other interests or hobbies. Here one needs a more balanced approach to life. It is not all about one's job or how much money one makes.

"So, when seeking work, or if you already have a job, it is important to keep in mind that a human being isn't meant to be some kind of machine designed only for production. No. Human life isn't just for work, like this communist vision where everyone's purpose is just to work for the state, and there is no individual freedom, where the state even arranges the person's vacations and everything is planned out for the individual. That is not a full human life. Individuality is very important for a full human life, and then accordingly some leisure time, a bit of holiday, and time spent with family or friends. That is the means to a complete form of life. If someone thinks only of money, at the expense of other human values, human good qualities . . . no, no, no!" he repeated emphatically. "If your life becomes only a medium of production, then many of the good human values and characteristics will be lost—then you will not, you cannot, become a complete person.

"So if you're looking for work and have a choice of a job, choose a job that allows the opportunity for some creativity, and for spending time with your family. Even if it means less pay, personally I think it is better to choose work that is less demanding, that gives you greater freedom, more time to be with your family, or to do other activities, read, engage in cultural activities, or just play. I think that's best."

As always the Dalai Lama ended on a practical note. But it's not always easy to practice the practical. Few would disagree that it's best not to invest our whole identity in our jobs, but it's not always easy to follow that advice.

Years ago, while I was still practicing psychotherapy, a formerly powerful CEO in the media industry presented for treatment with a full set of the classic symptoms of depression: fatigue, insomnia, loss of appetite, anhedonia, dysphoria—the complete picture of a depressed man, one who had lost interest in everything and was plagued by feelings of worthlessness, of hopelessness. He was an expensively dressed, distinguished-looking man, appearing much younger than his seventy-two years, but his unshaven and unkempt condition left a distinct, unmistakable stamp of depression on his countenance.

Speaking in a low monotone voice, he described how, starting at the bottom, he had built a hugely successful media corporation, but he had recently decided to quit. His company had been sold to a large multinational conglomerate a few years before, and while he had made a fortune from the sale, he had also requested to stay on as CEO to run the company. But after a couple of years, he became increasingly disenfranchised as major decisions were gradually taken out of his hands. Finally, the parent company made an acquisition that he felt "impinged on the bottom line of my division," and feeling his status and power slipping away, he decided to quit.

This man's diagnosis was clear and straightforward, and it was easy to identify the significant "psychosocial stressor" that had triggered his major depression: the loss of his role at work had been an assault to his self-identity. The treatment plan was equally clear: assist him with the process of adjustment while at the same time helping him recognize and embrace the many other aspects of his life that have played a significant role in shaping his sense of self, his identity. *Piece of cake,* I thought after eliciting further details about his history. His tremendous social resources and many other facets of his life could be nurtured and cultivated. He was a husband, a father, a grandfather. He had been actively involved in a number of charitable organizations, still sitting on the advisory board of more than one, and until the depression caused him to curtail his customary pursuits, he had been highly motivated in his involvement. He had even taken a part-time teaching post at a prestigious university.

After several sessions, however, it became obvious that the therapeutic intervention wasn't going to be as easy as I had initially anticipated. Session after session he continued to indulge in nonstop rumination and complaints about his former colleagues and the poor state of his industry. He continued to focus solely on his former position, to the exclusion of the other aspects of his life. It was apparent that I had underestimated the degree to which his self-identity was tied to his job and the status and power that went with it.

Of course I made a well-intentioned attempt to help him expand his self-concept and look at all the other areas of his life, to help him appreciate the richness and bounty that life had provided him. But largely without success. The medication I offered him resolved his symptoms of depression within a matter of weeks, and his energy level, concentration, appetite, and sleeping patterns all returned to their former levels. But there is a difference between happiness and the mere absence of depression. And after a lifetime of investing his identity in his work, he was never able to let go and transfer his identity to the other potential sources of fulfillment in his life. At least not during the period that I saw him.

Fortunately, however, there is still hope for most of us, particularly if we start ahead of time and don't wait until the end of our career to cultivate a wider sense of who we are. All it takes is willingness, attention, and a bit of effort, and each one of us has the capacity to develop stategies to expand our self-identity beyond the workplace.

Not long ago, a friend of mine, Lena, described a method she has been using for some time to overcome her fear of job loss and help to extricate her personal identity from her role at work. "I got to a point in my career where my whole life revolved around my job. I was up when things were good and down when things were bad at work, and my social life took a backseat. As I progressed, and got promoted a bunch of times, things became more competitive and if you lose a job at that level, it's much harder to find a comparable one. I found myself having difficulties sleeping and becoming short-tempered because I was so worried about losing my career. I was having full-blown anxiety attacks over it. I had lost myself, and something needed to be done. I needed a way to unhook my identity from my work. So I began to rehearse every day in my mind what my life would look and feel like if I were fired. I visualized what the meeting with my boss would be like when I got canned, and thought about how my colleagues would treat me afterward (like I had the plague, I'm sure), whether people would remain my friend or drop me like a hot potato once I had lost my high-status job.

"I would think about what it would be like to find another job, and what it would be like if I were shut out of my industry and had to go back to waiting tables or something like that. After years of consistently doing this, I began to realize that though I may lose status and income, I would still be able to find ways to support myself, and I began to relax. I remembered that my roles as friend, sister, wife, aunt, and mentor to younger people were equally important. In fact, I thought a lot about all the other things that make life worthwhile. You know, I think it even made me more creative on the job," she told me. "Since I was no longer afraid to lose my job, I was more outspoken and willing to take chances that ended up really paying off."

Of course, Lena isn't alone. For many of us, the demands of our jobs, are so consuming that it's sometimes easy to lose sight of what makes life worthwhile. But it's worthwhile to remember what's worthwhile, and like Lena we may need to remind ourselves of this consistently, before we end up investing our whole identity and purpose for living in our role at work.

Some might consider tenured college professors or U.S. Supreme Court Justices to be nature's final word in job security, but compared to the Dalai Lama these individuals are hanging on to their jobs by a thread. Not only is he assured of his position as Dalai Lama throughout his lifetime, but he is guaranteed the same job in numberless future lifetimes as well. That's job security.

Yet despite his celebrated and highly conspicuous role as a world spiritual figure, leader of the Tibetan people, or Nobel Peace Prize laureate, I knew from many past conversations that he identifies most strongly with his role as "a simple Buddhist monk." Based on years of observation, I've come to the conclusion that he is a genuinely humble man, one who has somehow managed to avoid getting caught up in the outer trappings of his title or designation as the Dalai Lama, one who truly sees himself as just an ordinary monk.

Since it seemed that his personal identity was tied to his role as a monk, at least to some degree, and since we had been discussing issues related to job loss, and to work and identity, a question occurred to me: I wondered how he might react if somehow he suddenly had to give up his "job" as a monk. Of course, this was a purely theoretical question—in reality, it was virtually impossible to imagine. But by now I was accustomed to the occasional bit of good-natured needling about my impossible or silly questions, so I was not deterred from inquiring.

"You know, in the past we've spoken about personal identity. You've mentioned that there can be many levels to an individual's self-identity, but in your case out of all of your various roles you seem to relate most strongly to your role as a monk. In a sense that role seems to be more fundamental to your identity than your designation as 'the Dalai Lama.' For example, you once told me that even in your dreams you see yourself as a monk. . . ."

He nodded. "That's right."

"Just for the sake of argument, then, can you imagine a situation where you lost your job as a monk? In other words, let's say that you could still do your daily meditation and spiritual practices, and lead a life of simplicity and so on, but you couldn't wear your robes or engage in any rituals as a monk, and you couldn't be part of the monastic community. And let's say that you had to earn your living doing something else to support yourself. Can you imagine how you might adapt to those kinds of circumstances? What type of work would you want to do?"

Knowing the unlikelihood of the Dalai Lama hitting the pavement to seek new work, I braced myself for a bit of gentle ribbing about my tendency to ask "irrelevant," "impossible," or "silly" questions. But to my surprise, he seemed to take the question very seriously. In fact, the expression on his face was uncharacteristically grave (well, almost grave), as he nodded thoughtfully and replied, "Yes . . . now, just recently in fact I was reading a Tibetan text by a great Buddhist master who lived in the late nineteenth and early twentieth century, and in this text he was giving advice to his students. He told them that it is important for them to understand what is the true essence of spirituality. He advised them that, recognizing the true essence of Buddhist practice, they should not get caught up in the external forms of practice like reciting mantras, making circumambulations, making prostrations, and so on. Of course, these are aspects of Buddhist spiritual practice, but they are not the core. The core of Buddhist practice really is to bring about inner transformation, through spiritual training of the mind. And I think one can still practice the essence, the core, even without the external forms.

"This author then went on to encourage those students with the greatest capabilities, those who hold the highest spiritual ideals, to live as hermits in the wilderness, in solitude. He cited extensively from the very inspirational 'songs of experience' written by Milarepa. As I was reading this, I was very moved by some of the passages, particularly some of the passages where it says one should 'live in indeterminate places, living single-pointedly, with a single-pointed dedication to meditation practice,' and so on. When reading this text, I was reminded of when I was younger, when I had a great yearning and felt very much drawn to the ideal of living as a hermit, living, as a Tibetan expression says, 'like a wounded animal withdrawing into solitude.'

"Of course," the Dalai Lama continued wistfully, "even though reading those passages reawakened that yearning, I immediately realized that now I'm in my middle sixties. Much time has passed. And also with this title of Dalai Lama I have many responsibilities. And I thought that even if I were to choose that kind of life, living in solitude, I don't know if I would have the skills to cook for myself, even make myself a cup of tea." He chuckled. "And on top of that I thought about many practical considerations, questions of security, what I would do if someone came to harm me. So all of these things would make it harder for me to live as a hermit at this point in my life."

The Dalai Lama was perfectly still for several moments, lost in his private thoughts, maybe pondering the course of his life, I don't know. But he soon roused himself from his reverie and added, "Anyway, if I had been younger and my situation in life had been different, that is what I would have liked to do. Your question reminded me of these things. And to answer your question about choosing an alternative kind of job or life if my situation was different, living in solitude as a hermit is the only thing that comes to mind. Apart from that, I have no other ideas; the thought never occurs to me."

At the time of this conversation, I had a sense that the Dalai Lama's situation and circumstances were so unique that very little of what he said could be applied to the rest of us. After all, even ignoring his position as the world's only Dalai Lama, few of us are monks, and fewer still would consider being a hermit as the only alternative to their present employment. Reviewing our conversation in my mind later on, however, I was less certain about the lack of relevance of his thoughts to the rest of us. A key idea emerged: *distilling the essence of one's particular role or activity, and binding one's identity to the essence rather than the outer trappings of one's position.* In the Dalai Lama's case, the work of a monk is spiritual practice. The external activities or duties of this job involved certain rituals, recitations, a certain manner of dress and behavior. The essence involved inner development. He made it clear that even if he had to relinquish the external forms, he could still be happy by retreating into solitude and continuing to practice the essence.

Perhaps this was something that could be applied to others after all. The earlier example of Lena illustrated how a person can discover techniques to expand one's self-concept beyond the confines of the workplace. In her case, she found that visualization and mental rehearsal of her worst fears coming true, along with deliberate reflection on the various roles she played in life, her non-work-related roles, was an effective strategy to divest her self-identity from her job.

But in regard to discovering effective strategies, it seems that the Dalai Lama added another dimension, taking a quantum leap, in fact. In a sense one could conceptualize Lena's technique as widening one's self-image by "outward expansion"—looking out across the landscape of her life to find other parts of herself beyond the workplace. These other roles may be related to relationships—spouse, parent, child, sibling, or friend—or to activities—hobbies, interests, athletic endeavors, volunteer work. The Dalai Lama's method, on the other hand, involves widening one's identity by a kind of "inward expansion"—going to the core, moving to a deeper and more fundamental level by discovering the essence of the particular role or activity. From this perspective, then, the essence of one's role as a spouse, parent, or friend is human love and affection. The essence of one's hobbies, such as studying a new language or learning new cooking recipes, could be the love of learning. The essence of other interests, such as painting or sculpting, might be an appreciation of beauty. Or the essence of athletic pursuits, such as golf or basketball, might be the exercise of skills or cultivation of good health. In this sense, the essence of one's job might be to assure survival, of course, but it may also involve making a meaningful contribution to others or to society in some way.

It would seem reasonable that basing one's identity on the essence rather than the external form would decrease the likelihood that one would be devastated by the loss of any particular role or job—after all, the essence is portable and can be transferred to any activity, any given relationship, hobby, or job.

Yes, the more I thought about it, the more this seemed to be a sensible approach to preventing the destructive consequences of investing too much of one's identity in one's job. Still, I wasn't entirely certain about how effective this method might be or how easily it could be done. I guess I'll have to give it some more thought. Perhaps give it a try myself.

Chapter 8

RIGHT LIVELIHOOD

Not long ago, I had lunch with a friend, a young actor. Like most actors he is poor and struggling, still looking for his first major role.

"I really love acting," he declared with animation. "Of course, I'm not making any money from it, but I wouldn't give it up for anything. It's my whole life."

Clearly my friend had found his calling. Lucky. "What do you love about it?" I asked.

"It's all about expressing yourself."

"Expressing what?"

"Whatever. Expressing your emotions—in my craft, I can use everything I've ever experienced, anything I've ever felt, and there's nothing like standing on stage and expressing that to others. It's a great feeling."

Our conversation reminded me of when I was younger and

wanted to be an artist. I spent four years in art school, loving every minute of it, eventually receiving a university degree in art. In those years, I became quite adept in drawing and printmaking, but conceptual art was my primary interest. My preferred medium was found objects, which I spent long hours sawing, gluing, stapling, sewing, and welding into elaborate assemblages, immortal sculptural masterpieces—at least they were in my own mind. I wasn't a stranger to the flow state either, becoming so absorbed in my work that I often lost track of time, working late into the night. When not immersed in creating a print or sculpture, I'd spend time in coffee shops or bars with my fellow artists, all of us filled to the gills with bonhomie or bourbon, bellowing out rambling litanies about art and life, each of us seeking to create our own unique mode of expression. And of course our uniquely original style was heavily influenced by other artists, who were influenced by others, who were influenced by others. Our world was very insular, our work replete with vague references to cultural trivia, or satirical references to others' work, or obscure inside jokes, but definitely full of hidden meaning—so hidden in fact that it was hidden from ourselves.

I was thrilled one year when one of my works was selected for a juried art exhibition. Proudly poised by my work the opening night, I was anxious to hear others' assessment of my art, standing by for the accolades that were sure to come.

One stout elderly woman sporting Coke-bottle glasses, a faded print shift, thick-soled shoes, and carrying a large nylon net shopping bag, stopped to look at my piece in silence for a long while. She had a slightly quizzical expression on her face, as if she had gotten lost on her way to Bingo and couldn't quite make out how she had landed here.

"You the artist?" she asked pleasantly.

"Yup."

Nodding toward my masterpiece, she said, "What does it mean?"

"Nothin' really. It's just something I made up."

I wasn't lying. Like most of my artist colleagues, none of us really started with a coherent message or meaning we were trying to convey. It was not meant to instruct or uplift. Our work was merely a collection of images that for one reason or another struck some chord in us. The meaning came later—whatever meaning an observer wanted to ascribe to the piece was up to them: A powerful commentary on post-modern existential valor in the crusade against the incessant groans of angst-ridden cranky Belgian dust mites. The eternal radical interplay between the positive and negative space of polar corn husks. A really cool yellow thing on top of that orange fuzzy thing. Who cares? The most that the artist could hope for was to elicit some emotion from the viewer. The specific emotion didn't really matter—it could be inspiration, joy, laughter, sadness, anxiety, fear, disgust, or anger. Take your pick. It made little difference—although disgust or anger were popular favorites in my day.

The lady continued, "Can I ask you a question?"

"Sure."

"Well, I really like your . . . uh . . . *thing.* I mean, it's interesting and all . . ."

I was all ears.

"So don't get me wrong," she continued, "but I'm just wondering—does this really help anybody? I'm just wondering, what's the point?"

Not a question to inspire great affection for the woman, and one that would normally put an artist on the defensive. And it was a question to which I had not given a great deal of thought.

"Umm . . . I dunno." I shrugged helplessly. "But I'm glad that you liked it," said I, fleeing as if she had the Ebola virus.

It was not long after that that I gave up art to pursue a career in medicine.[9]

Throughout our series of conversations, at least up until our last meeting, we had focused primarily on examining our underlying attitudes toward the work we already have. But having raised the issue of losing and choosing a job, we had shifted from an internal to an external orientation—and in today's session I felt compelled to expand on that topic with the Dalai Lama, to look deeper into the nature of the work one does and the impact it has on the world around us.

"Yesterday, you mentioned some of the factors one should take into account, at least if it's possible, when choosing work. Today I'd like to continue with the discussion about choosing one's career, the attitudes toward one's work that takes into account the specific nature of the work one does.

[9] Lest I offend those working in the arts, I should point out that as the years have passed I have come to recognize and appreciate the significant contribution of the arts to our society and to the world.

"Now, throughout most of human history people had very few choices about the type of work they did. They were born and basically they did what their parents did, maybe farming, herding animals, or became some kind of craftsman. So, historically they didn't have many choices, they were usually born into a particular line of work. That started to change around the sixteenth century in Europe, as young people began abandoning the farms and headed for the cities. People began to have choices about the work they did, and that kind of change has rapidly escalated over the past five hundred years. Today in the West, there is a tremendous variety of jobs. Of course, in many parts of the world, there are millions or even billions of people who still have very little choice, people who live in rural areas and in some of the poorer nations. But in the industrialized nations and in urban settings at least, there is a vast array of employment choices.

"Now, this may be changing somewhat over the past couple of decades, but still, when people are presented with the choice of several different jobs, often they tend to simply choose the one that offers the most money. That is the prime consideration. Yesterday you mentioned a few other factors that one might take into account when choosing work—factors such as choosing a job that may pay a little less but at least allows some free time with family or friends. So my question to you is, do you feel that there are any additional factors that people should take into account when choosing the type of work that they go into? Factors which you may not have mentioned yesterday?"

Taking a moment to sip some tea, the Dalai Lama responded, "If a person has a choice of the kind of work they do, then generally speaking of course it is best if the person chooses work that fits well with their particular disposition and temperament. Now here, self-understanding is required, self-awareness. We talked about this the other day. So as I mentioned, a person will also feel less frustrated at his or her job, more satisfied, if they have an accurate assessment of their knowledge of the field, their skills and technical abilities, to make sure that they have the right qualifications."

"Yes, that's true," I agreed, "and in this regard there are also career counselors who can help people find out what their natural talents are, what type of work they might be good at. But what I'm wondering is, from your personal perspective or perhaps from a Buddhist perspective, are there other considerations besides things like salary or one's personal strengths that a person should take into account when choosing a job, to assure a deeper or more long-term happiness at work?"

"Oh, yes," he responded immediately. "It may be difficult to apply to everybody, but one factor that would be very useful to consider is the benefit or harm caused by the work that one does. Now, from a Buddhist perspective, we talk about the concept of 'right livelihood.' The Buddhist concept of right livelihood means that you strive to engage in an activity that has no potential for being harmful to others, either directly or indirectly. The wrong means of livelihood is often described as any means of livelihood that involves exploitation of others out of negative motives, such as deceitfulness and guile. In wrong livelihood, you grab things to which you have no particular right. You take things from others. From a layperson's perspective, if the livelihood that he or she engages in has no direct or indirect harmful consequences for others, then that could be seen as a right livelihood. What the Buddha seems to have emphasized is ensuring that when you seek your livelihood, you do so in an ethical way; you don't harm others, you don't damage others, and you don't act with deception or guile. He seemed to be more concerned about the way in which you go about making a living rather than how much money you make."

"You mention the importance of assessing the potential benefit or harm of the kind of work you do," I recapped, then added another twist. "Now, the other day you mentioned that one means of turning your work into a calling was to analyze the broader contribution of your job. Let's say an individual is getting bored and they decide that they are going to systematically review the broader implications of their work. Instead of just sitting on an assembly line, pushing a button all day, they start to contemplate what their actions contribute to society so that they can feel more enthusiastic about their job again, feel better about it. So they start analyzing, but then they discover that the type of work they are doing is ultimately harmful for the environment. Or let's say they make a part that is used for weapons. Once they think about it, they realize that it is not productive—in fact, it's destructive in some way. And yet at the same time, maybe they don't have a lot of resources—they can't just quit their job and look for a better job because they have a family to support and there aren't many other industries in their area. I'm wondering if you could address that issue in view of your definition of 'right livelihood.'"

The Dalai Lama was quiet, instinctively running his hand over his shaven head as he turned the dilemma over in his mind.

"This is a very complicated question. There are so many factors at play here, it is very difficult to come up with a definitive approach to this question. On the one hand, if your work turns out to be part of weapons production, if you look at the immediate purpose of a weapon, then you will come to realize that this is for destruction, this is for killing. But at the same time if you look at the picture from the vantage point of overall society, unless there is a fundamental change in the society as a whole, for defense purposes for the society, or even on the global level, nations do need weapons for security purposes. Especially in the American case, you look at the fact that in the world there are totalitarian regimes who are against democracy. I think so long as those nations are there, the American military power must remain. But then again if the President used American military power for destruction or elimination of a single individual, the leader of a dangerous totalitarian regime for instance, I don't know if this is really appropriate or not, I don't know. It's a very complex problem.

"The question is, how will a given individual relate to this problem, and that is a very complex issue. Because on one hand, yes, weapons production is destructive; but on the other hand, for the well-being and the global security of the world as a whole, nations do need weapons.

"And for example, there are Western European nations who produce weapons, but use them mainly for defensive purposes and do not abuse them. And similarly, the example of the United States, although the Russian threat is no longer there, so long as a totalitarian regime like China exists with a huge military power, some kind of deterrent power is necessary. Then again there is a question whether the leaders of these countries will act responsibly in the use of the military power they have at their disposal. All of these are very complex issues. For an individual who comes up with moral qualms about being part of this company or this factory, and to what extent it is wise for him to give that job up, and how effective that is, is open to question. Whether that individual decides to quit or not to quit may not make a difference. It's a bit like the story of this old Tibetan woman inside Tibet who was so cross with the Tibetan government, it is said she turned her back to the government for a couple of years in protest—which didn't really have any practical power or effect."

"So you're saying that it would be acceptable then for them to keep their job, recognizing that their quitting and losing their livelihood isn't going to have an impact in the long run?" I asked, with a note of surprise. Was he advocating people continuing to work in morally questionable jobs?

"It's very tricky, Howard. I can't say what any given individual would do. Of course, it will depend very much on the individual. There are some individuals who may have stronger restraints coming from their religious faith. This is very tricky, even for a Buddhist, one who of course has taken certain vows of nonharm. Say an individual is a Buddhist, and clearly it is ethically better for that person to recognize the potential destructiveness of the action he is part of. Now then, to take the next step, which is to quit, and of course if there is a realization that simply by quitting it's not going to make any difference, then for the individual to quit and face the consequences of the family suffering in their livelihood and so on—all of this has to be weighed in.

"So, before we were talking about the case where a person is able to choose the kind of work they do, and therefore choose work that does not harm others, either directly or indirectly. O.K. But this is a case where a person may already have some employment but later discover that the job might indirectly cause harm. So there you need to take it on a case-by-case basis, and take into account all the variables, the nature and the degree of the harm, the person's values, and so on. So, that's where individual differences come in."

I wondered about cultural differences as well. "Just as there may be individual differences in people's attitudes toward work, from your experience, do you feel that there are cultural differences? Are Eastern or Asian attitudes different from Western attitudes? Or, for example, do Tibetans view work differently than Americans or Europeans or other cultures?"

"First, I think that it is dangerous to overgeneralize," the Dalai Lama reminded me, "saying that all Easterners are one way and Westerners are another, as if all people from a region are the same. But having said that, of course, just as there are individual differences, there may be local, national, regional, and cultural differences in people's attitudes toward work. This may affect satisfaction with one's job. For example, in India there is work, such as serving in restaurants, that is seen as demeaning labor, and this attitude is true for Tibetans who live in India as well. I've known some Tibetans who were working in government offices who would never even consider working in a restaurant here. But then they immigrated to the States, and there they were willing to work even in a restaurant as a dishwasher, and they were perfectly happy. Apparently they only felt embarrassed when other Tibetans came into the restaurant. This is because that kind of work is not seen as so demeaning in America, so this shows how the surrounding culture can affect satisfaction with one's job."

"Well, I'm not sure about that lack of bias against certain jobs in America," I said. "I think even in the States, there are cultural attitudes and biases against certain types of work. To a large extent, you're judged based on the status of your job."

"But it is much worse in India," he contended. "There is much more bias against that kind of work. And I think in America, in that kind of capitalist society, one is judged more on the amount of money one makes rather than the precise nature of the job itself. So, if dishwashers normally made large amounts of money, it would not be considered demeaning. Money is the determining factor. In India or other countries, there may be a bias against the nature of the work itself, being in a serving position. I think the emphasis on freedom and equality in America reduces the prejudice against those kinds of jobs to some extent, as long as it is honest work. So there, it is the human being that is more important than the job. For example, when I went to see former President Jimmy Carter at his home, apart from one guard outside, inside he was very simple, very down to earth, he was doing his own household things, cooking and all the others. Or when I visit President Vaclav Havel in the Czech Republic, at his home he is very humble, he answers his own door, and so on. In India it would be almost impossible to even imagine a former president of the country doing those things. They would have servants doing all these things. Cooking, making your own cup of tea, or that sort of thing would be seen as too demeaning for a high government official in India. So it is a cultural attitude.

"And I think even within the same region, within Asia, for instance, you can see cultural differences. Japanese, Chinese, or Tibetan attitudes toward work may all be different. For example, nowadays inside Tibet, you can see differences between Chinese attitudes and Tibetan attitudes. The Chinese seem more preoccupied with money, whereas a Tibetan may take money for his services, but may also accept some *chang*[10] or other things in payment. Take a Chinese tailor and a Tibetan tailor. Both have to make money to live, but you might see the Chinese tailor working day and night, trying to make money, money, money. But I think generally among Tibetans, money isn't as important. They may sacrifice earning more money so they can have more leisure time, time with their family, and so on. Of course, the Chinese worker might become rich, but even though they may not become rich the Tibetans don't seem to have much enthusiasm for sacrificing their time with family and other things just to make more money. Their view of life is based more on overall contentment.

"I think it is good that you raised the issue of cultural differences, because the approach to dealing with one's job, the attitudes toward work, and the nature of employment may vary from one culture to the next. These differences may be deeply

[10] Traditional Tibetan barley beer.

ingrained in the culture. For example, on one hand, I think in warmer climates where there may be an abundance of fruits and vegetables, where the weather is good and it is easy to grow crops, the people may take a more relaxed approach to life. They may place more emphasis on leisure time and have shorter working hours. On the other hand, in a colder climate, under harsher conditions, where survival is more difficult, this may have eventually given rise to cultures that placed much greater emphasis on hard work. In those northern climates and under those conditions, they had to find new ways to help survival, so they may have developed sea routes, and eventually industry, science, technology, and these things. At least that is my belief.

"Anyway, in our discussions here, it is important to keep in mind that we are discussing work more from the standpoint of modern industrialized societies. From that perspective, some of the issues we are addressing may not really fit in a different society—for instance, in traditional Tibetan society."

"Well, even though some Western attitudes toward work may not apply to Tibetan society and vice versa, I'm still wondering if certain aspects of the Tibetan attitude about work or certain practices might be applied to our society and become useful in the West. For example, you mentioned the Buddhist concept of right livelihood. Tibet was a thoroughly Buddhist country, so I'm wondering how those principles were integrated into that society—for example, the practice of choosing work that was not harmful. I assume that was a prime consideration when choosing one's work?" I asked.

"In the traditional society, most people automatically did the types of work their families did, the types of work I mentioned—

nomads, farmers, merchants, and so on. But some people still engaged in work that was not in keeping with the principle of nonharm, because there are butchers, metal smiths who make swords, and so on. But these kinds of work were also generally hereditary."

Resisting his invitation to dispel my vision of the perfect Shangri-la, where everyone was merrily engaged in beneficial, nonviolent work, I continued, "Speaking of work and the implementation of the concept of nonharm, there was a fascinating fact that I read in a book that was based on conversations with you—in fact, you mentioned it in two different books—that there was a rule in Tibet that any new invention had to guarantee that it was beneficial or at least not harmful for at least seven generations. . . ."

The Dalai Lama registered surprise. "I haven't heard about that."

It was my turn to be surprised. "That isn't true? It was attributed to you."

He shrugged and laughed. "I don't know who did that book, but maybe it was one of the so-called Tibetan experts. Some of these Western Tibetan experts know things even we Tibetans don't know. However, there do seem to be certain practices and policies that successive Tibetan governments adopted in Tibet that reflect putting into practice certain Buddhist ideals, such as the Buddhist principle of respecting the natural world, particularly the animal world. For example, all the communities living near the Yamdrok Lake used to rely heavily on fishing in the past. I used to believe that they were probably given exception to fish, but recently I heard about a policy that was adopted during the Fifth Dalai Lama's time, where they were discouraged from fishing, and in order to compensate them for that during a particular fishing season, some other communities would band together and provide them an equivalent value in grain, so that they would be compensated against their loss. Similarly, in the area near Mount Kailash, there is this Lake Manasarovar, and around Lake Manasarovar during a particular season, a lot of waterfowl migrate there. They lay their eggs on the shores and apparently there was again a government policy that during the egg-laying season, they would appoint people to watch over the eggs to make sure they were safe. Of course, there might be individuals who in addition to taking the salary probably ate some of the eggs as well. These things happen. But overall there is this kind of attitude of nonharm.

"So, even though in Tibet, people didn't always follow the principle of nonharm in their work—for example, there were butchers because Tibetans on the whole are meat eaters so some killing had to be done to supply the meat—this principle was still deeply ingrained in the people.

"In general, I think this is something that could be applied in the West. Although not everybody has lots of options about the work that they do, at least I think it is good to give serious thought to the kind of work one does, and the impact it has on others. And in the modern world particularly, and in industrialized nations where many people do have opportunities to choose the kind of job they take, I think it is best to choose work that does not cause harm to others, that does not exploit or deceive others, either directly or indirectly. I think that's the best way."

◆

• • •

Thus, the Dalai Lama added a final component to our quest for happiness at work, a critical factor from the Buddhist perspective—looking at the impact our work has on others, and assuring that we don't intentionally harm others in the work we do.

Earlier we spoke of the different attitudes one can adopt toward one's work, how those who view their work as a calling are clearly happier at work. Those who love their work, would continue to do it even if they didn't get paid (if they could afford to), who become absorbed in their work, who integrate their work with their values, their lives, their very being—these people have a calling. In addition, those with a calling see their work as meaningful, with a wider purpose, and ideally even contribute to the greater good of society or the world.

Despite this, from the Dalai Lama's perspective, merely viewing one's work as a calling isn't enough to assure our long-term happiness. Why? Imagine an expert computer hacker hard at work, breaking into secure systems to steal others' funds and sending out a few million computer viruses while he's at it. That individual may love what he's doing, spending long hours in the state of "flow," overcoming monumental challenges while utilizing every bit of his skill, knowledge, creativity, and ingenuity. Computers are his life, and his work may even perfectly mesh with his inner values—in this case, a value system based on the age-old philosophy, "Screw you, I'm taking what I can get! He who dies with the most toys wins!" And certainly there is a wider impact to his efforts, as he may wreak havoc in millions of lives as computers crash all over the world. This man has a calling. And for that matter so do many professional criminals, con artists, and others who get such a high from their activities that they would never consider doing other work unless forced to by the legal system or are fortunate enough to somehow undergo a major transformation of their outlook and inner values. One could even envision a guard at Auschwitz viewing his work as a calling, in his evil, distorted mind seeing his efforts as contributing to the greater good of the world.

There is no denying the fact that those who engage in work that deliberately harms others may enjoy some temporary feelings of satisfaction. But from the Dalai Lama's viewpoint, the states of mind that lead to destructive activities or harmful kinds of work, states of mind such as unbridled greed, hostility, anger, or even hatred, are simply incompatible with a person's long-term happiness.

Of course, the example of criminal pursuits or genocidal maniacs is the most extreme case, and as the Dalai Lama often points out, life is complex, and thus there may be varying degrees of harm or benefit that result from one's work, sometimes very subtle. But in assuring our long-term happiness, we can begin by cultivating some awareness of the impact of our work upon others.

Over the years, I've noticed that sometimes the Dalai Lama is asked to boil his philosophy down to a single fundamental principle. To this difficult question, he often replies, "If you can, serve others. If not, at least refrain from harming them." If we can do that on the job, we're well on our way toward happiness at work.

◆

Chapter 9

HAPPINESS AT WORK

Today was our final meeting in this particular series of discussions at the Dalai Lama's home in Dharamsala. We had spent the week exploring the nature of work, identifying some of the more common sources of dissatisfaction, and offering a few strategies people might use to make their work experience more satisfying.

As I trudged up the hillside, along the narrow muddy road leading to the Dalai Lama's home, past shopkeepers and tradesmen busily engaged in their daily tasks, I was reminded that whether here in India, or at home in Phoenix, many people spend half their waking hours engaged in work, some even more than that. But one question remained: Where does work fit into our overall quest for happiness? To what degree does work satisfaction affect our overall life satisfaction and happiness?

• • •

Embarking upon our final session, I reviewed, "This week we've talked a lot about work, about our attitudes toward work and some of the factors that can influence our happiness at work. Since today is our last meeting, at least for now, I wanted to talk about the link between work and happiness. In other words, what is the role of work, of productive labor, in achieving a happy life? To what extent does it contribute to our satisfaction and fulfillment? Here, I'm speaking about any kind of work, the general idea of productive activity, doing something that may help shape or impact the world around us."

"Very good," said the Dalai Lama, nodding his approval, "but I think if we are going to discuss work and productive activity, we first need to understand what we mean by productive activity. We should make sure that we have a common definition."

"That sounds like a good idea."

"So, if I understood correctly," he continued, "when you mentioned productive activity, you seemed to imply some kind of external activity. . . ."

"In a sense, yes."

"Now, from my point of view, inner development would be considered a productive activity. So this brings us to the question of how we define work. I'm wondering, what is your definition of productive activity?"

I hadn't thought about a precise definition of productive labor, and his question caught me off guard. Struggling to find the right definition, I didn't answer immediately, so he continued, "For example, I'm just an ordinary monk. Now this raises the question of whether the kind of work that I am primarily engaged in can be defined as 'productive' from the modern Western perspective. For example, many of my activities, especially those that pertain to my spiritual practice and my role as the Dalai Lama, would, at least from the Communist perspective, certainly be considered unproductive.

"So I'm just wondering about the Western attitudes toward a monk or nun, someone who really has good knowledge and is a sincere practitioner in his or her daily life—would you consider that to be productive work or unproductive?"

"Generally in the West, if there is a monk and all he does all day is sit in a cave and meditate, I think generally that would be considered unproductive work. To be honest, I don't know the precise or formal definition of what is considered productive labor or activity in the West. All I can do right now is speak from the perspective of an ordinary American and give you my impressions from a sort of popular perspective."

"Then I think we badly need a dictionary!" he joked, laughing.

"Anyway, from that perspective," I continued, "I think the general view of productive activity has to do with somehow making an impact in one's environment, producing something, or accomplishing something in the world. It seems to be more outer directed, accomplishing things that can be measured or quantified."

"So, in that case," the Dalai Lama laughed, "my few hours of meditation in the morning is unproductive, isn't it? And eating food, going to the toilet—unproductive."

"I suppose so." I also laughed, infected by his contagious sense of humor. "So what would be your definition of productive work?"

"Now that is a difficult question," he said pensively, rapidly shifting to a more serious frame of mind. "It can be quite complex. I think even from a conventional Western perspective this question can be a bit complicated. It may differ from one society to another and from one culture to another. For example, a communist society might consider the activity of communist propaganda, indoctrination, and so on, as productive, while a noncommunist society may reject these activities as unproductive. In fact, these activities may be seen as destructive."

He was silent for a while as he mulled it over. "So, you are saying, for example, my morning hours spent in meditation and spiritual practice may be considered unproductive by Western standards? This in fact reminds me of the Chinese Communist propaganda, where they extol certain kinds of hard work but the activities of a monk are considered unproductive. Yet am I right in thinking that if, as a result of my study and practice, I then engage in teaching or giving talks or lectures on those topics or participating in conferences, that would be considered productive activity—meeting with fellow human beings, engaging in conversations, and my teachings and lectures, these would be considered productive work?"

"Definitely," I replied. "Teaching is certainly a recognized profession in the West, so if a monk is studying and meditating and yet is teaching other people, that would be considered productive work. For example, there are people all over the world who are studying all these very esoteric disciplines, like they may study the life cycle of some obscure little bug, and that's still considered productive work because it's contributing to the general knowledge through teaching or writing articles.

"So, if you are applying your morning meditation and study in the world in some way, then it would be considered productive work because you're actually implementing it. But it wouldn't be if you were a hermit and didn't share it with anyone.

"Just to be clear," I added, "am I right in assuming that you would consider solitary meditation to be a productive activity? Would you consider to be productive our example of a monk who is a hermit, who has little contact with anybody else and spends his or her life just in meditation, trying to achieve liberation?"

"Not necessarily," he replied. "From my viewpoint, there can be both productive meditation and unproductive meditation."

"What's the difference?" I asked.

"I think many *dzogchen*[11] practitioners and other kinds of meditators practice different techniques, some with closed eyes, sometimes open eyes, but the very nature of that meditation is to become thoughtless, in a state free of thoughts. But in a way, this is a kind of retreat, like they are running away from trouble. When they actually face trouble, carry on their daily life and face some real life problems, nothing has changed. Their atti-

[11] *Dzogchen* is an ancient system of meditation practice in the Tibetan Buddhist tradition, dating back to the earliest development of Buddhism in Tibet. These meditation practices involve various techniques, including the cultivation of an experience of pure nonconceptuality.

tudes and reactions remain the same. So that kind of meditation is just avoiding the problem, like going on a picnic, or taking a painkiller. It's not actually solving the problem. Some people may spend many years doing these practices, but their actual progress is zero. That's not productive meditation. Genuine progress occurs when the individual not only sees some results in achieving higher levels of meditative states but also when their meditation has at least some influence on how they interact with others, some impact from that meditation in their daily life—more patience, less irritation, more compassion. That's productive meditation. Something that can bring benefit to others in some way."

Finally, a picture began to emerge. I said, "So it seems that your definition of productive activity, if I'm understanding correctly, is an activity that has a positive goal."

Once again, the Dalai Lama was quiet for a long while as he contemplated the matter. "From my personal point of view, yes. And not only a positive goal, but even if you have a positive goal, if your activity doesn't actually benefit anybody, I don't know whether or not that can be categorized as productive or not. For example, a person can study a lot. Read, read, read. Now, you may be reading an awful lot of pages, but if it doesn't produce anything or bring any benefit, then it is just a waste of your time. Of course, although that should be the general meaning of productivity, it still depends on the context. But generally speaking, if your activity or work can clearly benefit someone, I would classify that as productive. So, briefly put, I believe that a productive activity must be *purposeful* in that it is directed toward a specific goal. In addition, it must be an activity that is *beneficial* and not harmful to the well-being of the members of a given society.

"So, when one talks of 'productive,' from what we have discussed, I think generally, first one thinks in a material sense, something in the material field, something you can see, you can use—some kind of engagement or activity that produces some kind of material goods that people can use. Normally, production is equated with that kind of result. And second, many people think it may imply some positive thing. I think even in the conventional use of the word 'productive,' there is often a sense that there is a positive purpose—saying that someone is not being a productive person has a negative connotation. But then again, it is not always the case that some positive purpose or goal is implied in the use of the word. For example, one can talk of producing poison—it is productive, but it is negative. So there can be destructive actions, destructive work—it's called work and in one sense that too may be considered productive. Destructive work involves movement, movement toward something, creating new things. So in that sense it's productive, productive in the sense that it simply produces something.

"So generally I think the word 'productive' might be neutral, like 'work,' it can be either positive or negative. It is similar to the word 'freedom,' for example. I think freedom itself is not necessarily positive. You can be free to do negative things. Isn't it? But usually I think it is taken for granted that freedom is something good. So similarly, strictly speaking, productive is neutral: it can be either destructive or constructive, positive or negative, but usually we take it for granted that 'productive' is something that is not harmful. Maybe, but I don't know . . . I don't know." He laughed. "Again, I guess it really depends upon what exactly is meant by this word.

"Yes, this is complicated, complex. There are serious questions about the production of things like weapons or poisonous products. Of course, the employees who produce these things get a salary, sometimes quite a high salary, but if we characterize these activities as productive, we have to be aware of what sense of productivity we are using here. So again, we see the complicated nature of this issue. Say, for example, all the Nazi activity of genocide, which involved detailed planning, strategy, and implementation; we cannot say that these activities are productive. Similarly, criminals may be working hard but we would not want to characterize their work as productive either. So all of this suggests to my mind that in our conception of what is a productive activity, the concept of nonharmfulness, if not actual benefit to others, is somehow implied. Compared to these criminal activities, even if spiritual practices such as engaging in meditation may not have immediate material results, at least such activities are harmless, and so may be considered more productive. So, I don't know, conventionally speaking perhaps we can define productive work as an activity that entails production of something, either material or spiritual, that others can utilize and, through this, derive benefits from the activities that lead to its production. I don't know."

He suddenly started to laugh. "You know, we keep looking at different angles and different aspects of this idea of productive activity—productive, unproductive, positive, negative, various kinds and definitions of productive work, depending on one's point of view. It seems so complicated! Confusing! After all this, I'm wondering if we have come to any conclusions."

"I was wondering the same thing." I smiled. "I never expected that we would be wrestling with such a seemingly simple concept, trying to reconcile our different perspectives. But in fact I think the conversation may have had some benefit and made things clearer for me, because it changed my thinking in one regard. You asked me if I thought that meditating would be considered productive activity. From the conventional Western perspective, my initial response was no, but while you were talking I think I changed my mind. I want to recant my statement. Now I'm thinking that in view of your definition of productive meditation, where the meditative states are brought into the world, at the very least in how we interact with others, I think it would be considered a productive activity because the monks or meditators were learning, they were developing their minds, training their minds, and making positive changes. And in that sense they were making progress and accomplishing goals, so I think it would be considered productive.

"Anyway, I think we have come to an understanding. Even though different people may have different concepts of what they consider productive work to be, for the purposes of our discussions, I'd like to stick with your concept—that productive work involves being engaged in an activity that is associated not only with accomplishing something, some kind of goal-directed activity, but also that activity has to have some kind of positive purpose."

He nodded his head. "Agreed."

◆

. . .

After our discussion, I eventually did dig up a dictionary to look up the word *productive,* a word stemming from the word *produce,* from the Latin words meaning "to draw forward." There were no surprises—the English word has clear-cut creative and generative connotations, having to do with bringing forth, giving birth to a particular result, the creation of something. But simply taking a few moments to think about the definition of the word brought up an important point. As the Dalai Lama suggested, the term was essentially neutral—one could produce instruments of torture or one could produce a life-saving medicine—strictly speaking both would be considered productive activity. But from the Dalai Lama's perspective, a view of life that focuses on our quest for happiness, the mere production of goods or services is not enough to assure our ultimate happiness. For that to occur, one must add an additional element—we must also consider the results of our labor, the effect it will have on ourselves, our family, society, and the world. As we acknowledged in our discussion of "right livelihood," although it is not always easy, nor even always possible, we must do our best to assure that our work brings some benefit to others. For the Dalai Lama, that is the surest way to forge an unbreakable bond between our work and the deep and lasting happiness that we all seek.

For some who may consider redefining their concept of "productive labor," adopting the Dalai Lama's definition, there may be some danger involved. A cigarette salesperson, for instance, might no longer consider his or her hard work to be productive labor—at least according to this new definition. In fact, adopting this new definition may on the surface appear to be narrowing our definition, limiting the kinds of work that we would consider to be productive. But paradoxically, embracing this new definition of productive labor may actually expand our concept of productivity and open us to many new possibilities, many new sources of satisfaction at work. Changing our concept of productive labor can have some interesting consequences. Now, if we sell software and may have had an unproductive day in terms of not having had a single sale, we can still have a sense of accomplishment if we have had some positive interactions with our customers or co-workers, if we've made their day just a little bit better. Our day is now transformed into a productive day that we can take pride in. Of course, we still need to buy groceries and pay the rent, so all of us still need the conventionally "productive" days in which we generate some income from our efforts. But a wider definition of "productive labor," one based on being of some benefit to others, may provide us with many new sources of satisfaction that can sustain our sense of pride and accomplishment even during the inevitable slow periods of our career.

Having arrived at a common definition of productive activity, we were ready to take the final step—explore the link between productive activity and our fundamental yearning for happiness. The question remained: Do each of us have the inherent potential to experience a sense of deep satisfaction through our work, and if so, what role does work satisfaction play in our overall happiness in life?

Of course, as with most other facets of human behavior, evolutionary psychologists advance their own theory of why human beings have the natural capacity to derive pleasure and satisfaction from hard work:

On the savannas and plains of a primordial land in the distant past, there once roamed a small band of early humans. Among this band of prehistoric hunter-gatherers there were two brothers, Jim and Lemarr. Having common parentage and common characteristics as human beings, the brothers were similar in many ways. Both enjoyed squatting by a warm fire on a chilly night, enjoying a tasty haunch of antelope. But like all humans, there were subtle differences in their genetic make-up resulting in slight variations, not only in appearance, but also in intelligence, temperament, and disposition. Lemarr enjoyed making things, developing and exercising skills, and gained a sense of enjoyment and satisfaction from spending long hours engrossed in fashioning tools, which he could use to hunt and control the environment around him. Jim however, was less inclined to work, getting greater satisfaction from sitting around munching on walnuts and watching a sunset. One Tuesday afternoon, while he was engrossed in watching a caterpillar crawl across a leaf, Jim's career as a caveman was cut short as he ended up the featured item on the lunch menu of a saber-toothed tiger. Lemarr survived, and had several children who became our remote ancestors, and his trait of enjoying hard work was passed down to us.

Or at least so goes evolutionary theory. But regardless of the etiology, there is evidence to support the notion that human beings seem to be born with an innate capacity to get a sense of satisfaction from the work they do. In addition, there is a well-established relationship between a person's happiness at work and overall life satisfaction and happiness. Psychologists and social scientists first began to explore the relationship between work satisfaction and life satisfaction in the 1950s, and since that time, researchers have accumulated a massive amount of data confirming the link between happiness at work and overall happiness in life. In 1989, psychologists Marianne Tait, Margaret Youtz Padgett, and Timothy T. Baldwin reviewed the existing literature over the previous thirty years, and firmly established the link between work and life satisfaction. This link holds true whether one is a man or a woman, blue-collar or white-collar, whether one works on Wall Street or, as found in a recent study by Roderick Iverson and Catherine Maguire at the University of Melbourne, one works in a remote coal-mining community in Australia. Since the 1989 study, organizational psychologists, social scientists, and leading experts such as Robert Rice, Timothy Judge, and Shinichiro Watanabe have continued to examine the relationship between work and happiness, further refining our understanding of the nature of the relationship.

As one might intuitively guess, many investigators have proposed a "bi-directional spillover" model of job/life satisfaction. In other words, satisfaction with one's work tends to make one happier overall, and those who are happy with their life tend to be happier at work. Of course, as in most fields of research, there is some disagreement among researchers about the degree to which work influences overall happiness or to what degree a person's general happiness in life spills over into his or her job.

In looking at the link between work and life satisfaction, some researchers have even tried to quantify the relationship. A study of the quality of American life, funded by the Russell Sage Foundation, found that work satisfaction accounted for 20 percent of overall life satisfaction. In summarizing some of the literature on the subject, James Harter, Frank Schmidt, and Corey Keyes report, "As much as a fifth to a quarter of the variation in adult life satisfaction can be accounted for by satisfaction with work." While on the surface this may not appear to be a high number, when one takes into account all of the variables that may affect life satisfaction, including marital status, social supports outside of work, health, and other life circumstances, one can begin to appreciate the tremendous role that work can potentially play in a happy and satisfied life.

It seems clear that human beings have an innate ability to experience satisfaction through work, and further, there's a link between work satisfaction and life satisfaction. Lucky for us, since a major portion of our allotted time on earth is spent working. Still, it may require some effort to identify and remove the obstacles that prevent us from experiencing the joy at work that is our birthright. In our discussions, the Dalai Lama had offered an approach to beginning that process. But there was still something bothering me, still something missing. Noting that the Dalai Lama always seemed so happy no matter what activity he was engaged in, I had begun our discussions by questioning him about how he views his own work or job, in an attempt to discover what role work played in his own sense of fulfillment and happiness. My initial efforts in getting him to talk about his own job had proved fruitless, but now I thought it worthwhile to return to the subject once again. The question was how to approach the subject again in a way that would elicit a more complete response. A thought suddenly occurred to me as I remembered a brief exchange that had taken place the year before, while the Dalai Lama was in the middle of an intensive three-week speaking tour in the U.S.

It was the end of an exhausting day. The Dalai Lama was in the final moments of a public address, given in a large Midwestern city. As customary, in the final minutes of his talk, he was fielding the standard questions from the audience, ranging from "What's the current status of the political situation in Tibet?" to "Do you have a girlfriend?" Sitting on a folding chair backstage, I was on the verge of nodding off, when I suddenly became fully alert, startled by a question I had not heard before, a simple yet fundamental question that somehow I had failed to ask him during our many meetings over the years.

"You often speak about happiness," he was asked, "and you even claim that the purpose of our existence is happiness. So, I'm wondering, when was *your* happiest moment?"

The Dalai Lama was slow to reply, as if he had all the time in the world. When he finally answered, it was if he were chatting with a group of friends while drinking tea on the front porch of his home, instead of addressing thousands in a public arena, all of whom were eagerly anticipating his response.

"I don't know," he mused quietly, almost under his breath. "There have been so many happy moments, so many." Finally he laughed. "I think that perhaps it was when I passed my Geshe exams. I remember it was such a relief when it was finished, I was so happy!" Booming over the loudspeakers, his mirthful laugh resounded throughout the arena, reverberating in the hearts of each of his listeners.

I remembered how the Dalai Lama had responded to that question so cheerfully, and breezily dismissed the subject so quickly, that he left one with the impression of a young Dalai Lama sitting down at a Formica desk in a clean, temperature-controlled classroom, answering some multiple-choice questions and writing a few essays, handing in his blue book, and picking up his diploma on his way out the door. The reality of the situation was far different. The Geshe degree, akin to a PhD in Buddhist philosophy, is the culmination of seventeen years of hard work. It involves intensive study of many branches of Buddhist theory, logic, debate, and psychology. His field of study was riddled with arcane topics, and with courses so tough that I'd have to dust off my dictionary even to find out what the course title meant: "Let's see . . . epistemology . . . 'the study of the nature of knowledge.'" The oral exam lasted a full day, as Tibet's top scholars from the country's best monastic universities fired questions at him in front of thousands of monks and scholars. Added to this tremendous pressure for Tibet's young leader, the political situation in Tibet was so tense that for the first time in history there were armed guards, both Tibetan and Chinese, poised around the large courtyard, waiting for trouble to erupt at any moment. There had been a threat to his life, which he had been made aware of.

While one's happiness from passing a final exam is understandable, this wasn't what I would have thought of as a peaceful happy moment, and it was hard to imagine a situation more rife with internal and external challenges and pressures. Yet he claimed that this was his happiest moment, or at least one of them. To me, the implications of his response went beyond the idea of achieving a momentary sense of relief after overcoming a challenging and anxiety-provoking examination. It suggested a deeper link between hard work, sustained over a period of many years, and ultimate happiness and satisfaction.

Now, as I thought back to that question and his response about his happiest moment, it occurred to me that this might be the best way to address the link between work and happiness in his own life.

"When you were asked what was your happiest moment," I reminded him, "you said that it was when you finished your examinations and got your Geshe degree. I know that achievement took a tremendous amount of work over a period of many years. So, I think your response has some interesting implications. It implies that productive activity and meaningful work really are important components of human happiness, at least in your case. And that completely supports the findings of researchers and social scientists who find that in terms of a full human life, work is an important component of human happiness. In fact, some of these scientists feel that the brain may be hardwired—genetically programmed—to experience happiness through productive and meaningful activity, the exercise of skills, through interacting with and shaping our environment.

"So I find it really interesting that here, instead of saying my happiest moment was when I was sitting in solitary meditation one day or in some peaceful state of repose, you implied that it was related to hard work and accomplishing a certain goal on a conventional level."

The Dalai Lama appeared to be listening very attentively,

then responded, "I can understand your point that there is a certain amount of satisfaction from this idea of work. And in this case your description of productive activity relates more to the kind of externally oriented activity that we mentioned before. For example, when I was young, in Tibet, I used to enjoy fixing things, taking apart mechanical devices or objects like watches, and trying to understand how they worked, although I wasn't always able to put them back together properly. Sometimes I would even ignore my lessons so I could do these things." He chuckled guiltily. "But still, I don't think it is completely correct to say that human beings are genetically programmed to benefit only through this productive activity."

"Oh, no, no," I corrected. "That's not what I'm suggesting. In fact, the discussions that led to our first book were based on your premise that the primary determinant of one's happiness is the state of one's mind, the mental factor. Our first book focused on the general theme of inner development, and our current discussions already began with the assumption that inner development is what really brings happiness. So there is no question that we believe that.

"But you have also said that there are many components to human happiness. Here we are focusing on one of those elements, one that we did not fully explore in our first book. The additional element that I am bringing in here is the idea of productive activity and work. So, yes, I agree with you that we're not programmed to achieve happiness *only* through meaningful productive work or activity. But now I want to explore how work fits in to our quest for human happiness. And again, here we are not talking about elevated states of spiritual bliss, but about more conventional day-to-day and moment-to-moment happiness, and how productive activity and work can contribute to our overall life satisfaction—for example, how the hard work in getting your degree made you happy."

"There's one thing I should make clear," the Dalai Lama said. "By saying my happiest moment was getting my Geshe degree, I wasn't implying that profound states of happiness cannot be gained through inner development or the internal thought process gained through meditative realization. Now, although I may not have achieved those levels of meditative realization, that does not mean it is not possible. In fact, I have even had glimpses of that possibility. I think I have told you about some of these experiences in the past."

"Well, I think we can both agree that there are many components to human happiness," I allowed, "and many factors that can contribute to happiness. In the past, we've talked about the importance of training the mind, and you mentioned other kinds of inner meditative training. And of course there are things you've mentioned in the past, like family, friends, and so on. So some of these other components we can return to at a later date. But this week we have been focusing on work. We have discussed many aspects of work, livelihood, some of the common sources of dissatisfaction at work, and so on. Since this is our last meeting for this series of discussions, I'm wondering, from a broader perspective in terms of one's work, one's activity in the world, what role do you see that as contributing to our quest for happiness?"

The Dalai Lama thought awhile before answering. "It is very difficult to really say in general terms to what degree work plays a contributing role in human happiness. You know, there are still a lot of complex factors involved. The individual's interests, the background, the living conditions, the social setting, and the nature of the work can all affect the degree to which the person's work may contribute to their overall happiness. These can make a big difference. And I think to a large extent it also depends on the psychology, the psychological make-up, of the individual as well. So, if we are talking about the sense of fulfillment that individuals derive from the work itself, you have to understand that there are many factors at play."

I sighed inwardly. I recalled our many conversations over the years where I looked for clear-cut answers, definitive statements. Here we were again. Yes, once again here I was seeking sound-bite solutions and being offered nothing but unrelenting reminders of the complexity of human beings.

But he's right, of course. Although from a Darwinian perspective, we may have inherited from our remote ancestors an inborn propensity to experience pleasure and satisfaction from productive activity, we are no longer primarily a hunter-gatherer society. As humankind evolved into the modern world, life became more complex; for many, the spontaneous joy that we have the potential to experience through our work has become muddied by the complex variables that characterize life in the twenty-first century.

Earlier, we mentioned that while the general link between work and happiness has been established, there is considerable disagreement among researchers about the degree and manner in which work contributes to overall happiness. Despite this divergence of opinion, researchers and social scientists can at least agree on one thing: uniformly supporting the Dalai Lama's view that there are complex variables at play in determining one's satisfaction at work as well as one's overall satisfaction in life. As the Dalai Lama points out, the individual's personality, disposition, interests, social setting, and many other factors can all affect one's satisfaction at work. And as he suggested earlier, even one's national and cultural background can play a role, a fact that has been well documented by industrial and organizational psychologist Paul Spector in a recent book on job satisfaction.

Not only are there many variables or factors that can affect job satisfaction, there are also many factors that contribute to a happy life. As the Dalai Lama reminds us, job satisfaction is just one of those factors. There are many components to human happiness. Ed Diener, a professor of psychology at the University of Illinois, Urbana-Champaign, and one of the leading researchers in the field of subjective well-being, in looking at the extensive research on the factors that can influence human happiness, has concluded that it "seems likely that subjective well-being will not be accounted for by a handful of potent variables, because of the immense number of factors that can influence it." So, given the complexity of human beings, given the wide variety of biological, social, economic, or demographic variables that can affect our happiness at work or at home, where do we begin? Here, the latest scientific findings of researchers in the field of human happiness converge with the Dalai Lama's wisdom based on ancient Buddhist philosophy—we begin by turning inward, by reshaping our attitudes and outlook. Echoing the Dalai Lama's perspective, Dr. Diener concludes, "It appears that the way people perceive the world is much more important to happiness than objective circumstances." And there's a massive body of evidence to support that assertion.

Thus, despite the noble and well-intentioned attempt by some researchers to quantify the precise degree to which work contributes to our happiness, as the Dalai Lama suggests, it is difficult to generalize and it is largely an individual matter. And given the joy the Dalai Lama seems to exude as he goes about his daily activities, I was all the more curious about his personal perception of the work that he does. There was still something about his personal job description—"I do nothing"—that stuck with me, leaving me vaguely unsatisfied. I still sensed that by learning a bit more about how he views his own work and how his work fits into his life, that there was something that could be helpful to others—something that we could apply to our own work and to our own lives.

So, giving it one last shot, I said, "This week we've spoken about people's attitudes toward their work, the different views that people can have of their jobs. And I'm still curious about your own views of your work. The other day I asked what you would tell someone who asked you what you do for a living, and you said you'd tell them you do nothing, or joked that you just take care of yourself, and so on. But I'd still like to get more specific. I mean, in your case, you have various roles: you're an ordained monk, you're the leader of the Tibetan people, you're a statesman, a teacher, a Buddhist scholar, and you give talks and participate in various kinds of conferences all around the world. You're involved in lots of activities, so that's kind of what

I was getting at—what would you see as your work in the world? Your job?"

"Naturally, I'm a monk, I'm a Buddhist monk. So accordingly the work of a monk, or main interest, is the study and practice of Buddhism. And then the main thing is to serve others through spirituality, through my own experience. That's the main thing, isn't it? So, when I give talks, I'm trying to share with those people some understanding of what is beneficial, what is a meaningful life, according to my own experience.

"Now, if you are talking about my temporal work, my work in the world, my activities and my decisions are based on Buddhist principles. They are based on both the Buddhist concept of great compassion and the view of interdependence. For example, my Middle Way policy, my approach to the Tibetan political issue, is shaped by my view of interdependence, recognizing that in today's world all countries are interdependent. Naturally, for Tibet much depends on India, and much depends on China. So in that policy you also see the influence of Buddhist concepts such as nonviolence. We don't go to war with the Chinese to get our country back. So I think all my different activities are influenced by Buddhist concepts. Well, maybe not everything—I might do a little work with a screwdriver, and I don't know whether Buddhist concepts are involved there. I don't know"—he laughed—"otherwise I think the main or major part of my daily life is spent as a monk, as a Buddhist practitioner. So, for example, I'll wake up each morning at three-thirty and engage in study, prayer, and meditation. Of course, my brother teases me that I wake up so early because I'm hungry and want my breakfast." He laughed again. "That may be true, but I think the main reason is my practice. So, study and practice as a monk is my only profession. Otherwise, there's nothing else, zero."

"O.K.," I said, "but I know that you have many daily activities besides your spiritual practices as a Buddhist monk. You mentioned, for example, the political situation, and I know that you have duties and work related to your role as leader of the Tibetan people. To what extent do your other kinds of work, such as your political duties, contribute to your overall sense of happiness and satisfaction? Do you feel that it plays a role?"

The Dalai Lama explained, "There is definitely a correlation between the satisfaction that you achieve in the workplace and your overall sense of fulfillment. However, I am not sure whether my own personal experience here can be applied to the experiences of many other individuals. For example, this morning I was talking with some members of the Tibetan secretariat here and I was making the point that if, for example, we read Tibetan history, we see that through many generations we Tibetans have neglected the important changes going on around us so that we have now arrived at a point where much of the damage done is almost irreparable. So, in a way, my generation of Tibetans has inherited a crisis that has had tragic consequences for our culture and people as a whole. Yet at the same time, being a Tibetan, and especially being the Dalai Lama at such a critical juncture, provides me a tremendous opportunity to serve, to serve the well-being of a people and ensure the survival of its culture."

"So that seems to relate to what we had discussed about challenge the other day. You are saying that the greater the challenge, the greater the sense of satisfaction one might derive from work?" I asked.

"Yes, certainly. For example, in the case of my own responsibility for the Tibetan people and nation, as I mentioned, our present tragedy is in fact the result of many complex factors, including Tibet's own long period of negligence and ignorance of the events in the outside world. Yet when I recognize the gravity of the situation, the fact that the very survival of Tibetans as a people with their unique cultural heritage is threatened, I can then appreciate the value of even the smallest contribution I can make toward safeguarding the Tibetan people. This, in turn, reinforces my understanding of how my work in relation to the issue of Tibet is in actual fact part of my lifelong daily spiritual practice, the practice of someone who deeply believes that helping others is the highest goal of a spiritual practitioner. In this way, in my own life, my work becomes intimately connected with my daily prayer and meditation practice. For example, I find the use of analytical meditation helpful to generate deeper conviction in the principles of nonviolence, of compassion, of forgiveness, especially toward the Communist Chinese. So you see, there is a kind of mutual influence between my commitment to certain spiritual values, my daily spiritual practice, their impact on my overall thinking and attitude to life, and how these in turn affect my political work for the people of Tibet. Then, my political work influences my spiritual practice. In fact, there is an interconnected relationship between everything. If I enjoy a good breakfast, for instance, it contributes to my health. And if I enjoy good health, it's possible to utilize my life to carry on my work. Even a simple smile can have some impact on my overall state of mind. So, everything is interconnected, interdependent. When you appreciate the interconnected nature of all aspects of your life, then you will understand how various factors—such as your values, your attitudes, your emotional state—can all contribute to your sense of fulfillment at work, and to your satisfaction and happiness in life."

At last things fell into place. I finally understood how the Dalai Lama could claim "I do nothing" as his job description. Of course, I knew that with his lighthearted humor, there was a tongue-in-cheek element to this job description. And behind his joking about doing "nothing," I knew of his natural reluctance, which I have observed on many occasions, to engage in unnecessary self-appraisal. This seemed to grow out of his lack of self-involvement, absence of self-absorption, and lack of concern for how others view his work, as long as he had sincere motivation to be of help to others.

But there was a deeper truth here as well. As I had begun to understand during our discussion of personal strengths, he is someone who has completely fused his self with his work. His personal life and work life were perfectly integrated—so fully integrated, in fact, that there was no separation between his "personal" life, "work" life, "spiritual" life, or "home" life. And since he did not separate out a particular set of functions and relegate them to a "job" category, he had no job. "I do nothing." I have often marveled, in fact, at how he carries his full self with him wherever he goes—he seems the same in any setting. He has no "off-duty personality."

So, being fully present in every activity he did, the Dalai Lama had little need to modify or change his behavior based on the setting. He is who he is, the same whether he's at home or "at work." There must be an immense feeling of freedom in that kind of life, I mused. I thought back to an extraordinary scene I had witnessed the previous year. The Dalai Lama was visiting Washington, D.C., and one evening he attended a reception held in his honor at the Capitol building. The reception was given by Senator Diane Feinstein, and was attended by Washington's elite, a virtual who's who of Washington power brokers. The event was held in the richly decorated Appropriations room in the Senate side of the Capitol building. Ambassadors, high-ranking senators, and leaders of Congress glided silently across the plush red carpet, under ornate crystal chandeliers, surrounded by fresco-like murals in muted colors covering the walls and ceiling. The setting served as an appropriate backdrop to underscore the prominence of those present. I recognized many faces that I had often seen on television, but there was something unsettling about seeing these people in person. I wasn't sure why. Then, it occurred to me—many of these people didn't seem to be any more "live" than when I viewed them on TV. I looked closely at many of these leaders of Congress, their deeply lined faces frozen into an impenetrable mask, their movements stiff and automatic. And sprinkled in among them were eager young aides and interns, fresh out of college, intoxicated by the power around them, speaking with subdued excitement. *Trying to act grown up,* I thought. To me, someone with no prior exposure to the political world, the scene was almost surreal.

I had arrived early, and people were milling about. The older and more established guests seemed to be so secure in their positions, and so overwhelmed by their own self-importance, that they seemed to take little interest in anyone else. When they were introduced to someone, they looked right through them, barely acknowledging that there was another human standing in front of them. The younger or less secure, by far the majority, seemed to be equally oblivious to those they were talking to, as their eyes constantly darted about the room, trying to determine their place in the hierarchy of power. Some made their way through the crowd introducing themselves, and as I would later mention to the Dalai Lama, the most common question, was "What do you do?" They seemed to have a talent for sizing you up—within sixteen nanoseconds, they could determine if there was any way that you could be useful to them. If not, they were soon off, jostling their way through the room to meet someone more important. Some sipped on diet Cokes or white wine, and there was a long banquet table in the middle of the room laden with imported cheeses, fried shrimp, puff pastries, and assorted delicacies. The food remained largely untouched. Many appeared to be too tense to eat. I looked around the room and saw few who looked relaxed and happy.

Finally, the Dalai Lama entered the room. The contrast was striking. As usual, he appeared calm and cheerful. I noticed that he hadn't even bothered to put on his good leather Rockports—he was wearing his old rubber thongs. Senator Feinstein and her husband instantly began to introduce the Dalai Lama to some of the guests. He poured himself a glass of water while Senator Feinstein dragged a heavy antique dark oak chair across the room, pushing it against a wall and inviting the Dalai Lama to sit. Several senators lined up to be introduced. Standing across the room, I could not hear what they were saying, but observing the way that he engaged them—with a sincere handshake, warm guileless smile and direct eye contact—it was apparent that as always, he was relating to them just as one human being to another, with a complete lack of pretense. Soon there was the inevitable smile on the others' faces, even their posture relaxed. I noticed that after they were introduced, many of the guests lingered and seemed reluctant to leave. Finally, one senator pulled up a chair next to the Dalai Lama. The next in the receiving line did the same. Soon there were a dozen politicians seated along the wall, a half dozen on each side of the Dalai Lama. Observing how they leaned toward him attentively, engrossed in conversation, from across the room, the scene reminded me of the Last Supper. It seemed that the closer they were to the Dalai Lama, the more their faces and posture relaxed. Turning back a few minutes later, I was struck by an even more extraordinary sight—the Dalai Lama was affectionately holding the hand of the man seated next to him, a well-known seasoned old politician whom he had just met. He held the politician's hand as he would the hand of a small child, and the politician, who just moments before had appeared hard and impenetrable, suddenly seemed to visibly soften, suddenly seemed to become more human.

While this was taking place, I was chatting with the chief

State Department security agent in charge of the Dalai Lama's security. He had been assigned the same duty on some of the Dalai Lama's previous visits to the U.S., and told me that providing security for him was his favorite assignment—not only because unlike some of the other diplomats who wanted to go to discos until three in the morning, the Dalai Lama was in bed each night by nine, but also because he had a genuine admiration for him. He explained, "I'm not a Buddhist, of course, but the Dalai Lama really has inspired me."

"In what way?" I asked.

"I guess the main thing is that I've noticed that he likes to talk with the drivers, the janitors and waiters, the service staff wherever he goes. And he treats everybody just the same." There was no place that this was more evident than what I had just witnessed here at the Capitol. He treated all with equal respect. There was no difference between how the Dalai Lama treated the food server and the senate majority leader. His demeanor, his bearing, his speech, and his behavior were always exactly the same, whether he was speaking to the maid in the hotel, the driver on the way to a reception, or to the top politicians in the U.S.

So here was the answer—since he had no need for pretense, for acting a certain way in public or while "at work," and another way in private, and could just be himself wherever he went, this made his work seem effortless. Of course, most of us have a long way to go before reaching that level of integration, but the more we can reduce the gap between who we are and what we do, the more effortless our work will become.

EPILOGUE

The Dalai Lama's attendant, a tall gentle Tibetan monk wearing traditional maroon robes and a perpetual smile, quietly entered the room and began discreetly to remove the tea service. I realized that we were in the final minutes of our meeting. Knowing our time was coming to a close, I picked up my notebook and looked at the list of topics that I had hoped to explore with him.

Scanning the long list of topics that we had not yet addressed, I said, "We don't have much time left, but there are still many things I wanted to ask you about. I think we covered a lot of the things that cause people to be unhappy at work, but there are still some things we haven't covered—for example, the whole issue of ethics at work, the dissatisfaction caused when a person's personal values or ethical principles do not correspond with the ethical values of the organization where they work, the issue of whistle-blowers, the corporate scandals, and also I'd like to go into greater depth regarding interpersonal relationships at work and in business, both among co-workers and employer–employee relations, and—"

The Dalai Lama interrupted, "Howard, if you are going to get into a more detailed discussion of the workplace or specific problems that various individuals might encounter at work, then our discussion could be endless—after all there are six billion people in the world, and each one may have her or his unique problems. And also, here you are getting into another area. So far, we have been discussing happiness at work generally from the standpoint of the worker, the employee, and measures they can take to become more satisfied at work through their own efforts, by changing their outlook, increasing self-understanding, or the other things we talked about. But that is only part of the picture. The employer also, the management, the organization, all play a role in setting the tone of the workplace environment, and have an impact on the happiness of the employees, and of course if we are to discuss wider issues of ethics in business, the economy, and so on, that is another thing. . . ."

"Well, in fact I was hoping to move into a discussion of those precise areas, but I don't think we will have time now."

"So, that can wait for another time. Of course," he said, "I'm not sure how helpful I can be there, if I have anything useful to offer. I'm not an expert in business, I don't know much about it."

"Neither do I," I confessed, "but I know that you have a strong interest in applying secular ethics to all areas of human endeavor, and so I'd like to approach the subject from that angle, among other things."

"Of course, I am always willing to meet. So let us meet again, and exchange ideas, talk about these things and see what we can come up with. I will offer whatever I can. But I think that from your side, you should also investigate these topics on your own, do some homework. And it would be a good idea to talk with business people, experts in this field, and ask them to share their experiences, to see how they are implementing these principles in their companies, or the problems they encounter. So in this way, perhaps we can come up with something useful. We'll just do the best we can."

The Dalai Lama yawned, took off his glasses, and rubbed his eyes. It had been a long day for him. He reached down, slipped on his shoes, and began tying his shoelaces, the standard signal, based on past experience, that our meeting was coming to a close. "We've been discussing work, and this is part of our work. So, I appreciate your coming, I think you have come a long way from Arizona, your home. And I appreciate your sincerity," he said quietly as he finished tying his shoelaces and stood up. "So, thank you."

We have been discussing work, and this is part of our work. . . . Up until that moment it had not occurred to me to think of our meetings as work. Throughout our time together, it was as if we had been talking of work in an abstract sense, an activity that was occurring somewhere in the world as faceless, numberless masses went about their daily chores—certainly not something that was happening right there in the room. Of course, in the back of my mind I knew that at some point tremendous effort would be required if we were to shape our conversations into a book. That would be at another time, in another place. But these hours spent in discussion with the Dalai Lama were not work—I had been so engrossed in our conversations, so grateful for the opportunity to sit down with him and explore how I too might learn to become a happier person, that I would have paid to be there. This wasn't work. Or if it was, then somehow I had landed the same job as the Dalai Lama—"I do nothing." I guess the difference between us was that this was his permanent position and I was just a temp.

As I was getting ready to go, the Dalai Lama asked me to wait a moment and went into the side room of his office, emerging with a small Buddhist statue that he presented to me as a birthday gift. Not expecting a gift, I was so touched that I was speechless, and stammered out a few incomprehensible words of thanks. Then, standing on the porch by the screen door, the Dalai Lama smiled and gave me a long hug of farewell. We had spent many conversations grappling with human problems, the stuff of daily life, and ahead I had my work cut out for me, countless hours of editing, and at that moment of course it remained to be seen what would be the ultimate results of our endeavors. But at that instant, that moment of human contact, this simple exchange of warmth and affection with my friend and collaborator, I felt that this is what the work was all about.

APPENDIX

STABILIZING MEDITATION EXERCISES

The first stage in this exercise is to find an appropriate time and suitable place to practice; one that is as calm and peaceful as possible. Find a time when you know that you are not going to be disturbed for a period of at least five to ten minutes. If you wish, you can take your telephone off the hook or switch off the ringer. Or if you have a separate room, such as a study, where you know that you cannot hear the telephone, that is very good. Creating such a time and quiet space is important. Once you have successfully achieved the proper environment, then you can begin to undertake the formal sitting practice.

The next step is to assume the proper sitting position and posture. Sit in a position that is most comfortable. You can sit on a chair or on a cushion on the floor, or, if you find it more comfortable, you can even lie on your back on a bed, although in that case you should take care not to fall asleep. Whatever posture you adopt, it is crucial to keep your spine straight. Keep your arms in a relaxed position, your eyes slightly open, or you can keep them closed. If you choose to keep your eyes slightly open, your gaze should be directed downward, but without purposely looking at or focusing on any particular object. Your mouth should be closed but the jaw relaxed with the tongue slightly touching the upper palate just behind the top front teeth. It is important to ensure that there is no strain on any part of your body which might distract your attention.

Once you have adopted the correct posture, relax your shoulders while taking deep breaths. Then resolve that during this period of mental discipline you will try to retain the focus of your mind and will not allow it to wander aimlessly. This resolution is like setting the tone for a conversation.

Take a couple of deep breaths, and release them slowly. Breathe deeply from the abdomen such that the abdomen rises and falls as you breathe in and out. This breathing will help calm your mind and reduce the intensity of the constant thoughts that generally run through your mind. With this physical and mental preparation, you can then engage in the following exercises.

Exercise A

1. After taking the deep breaths—from three to seven depending on how many you need to reach a certain degree of settled mind—you should then return to breathing normally. Allow

the breath to flow in and out freely, effortlessly, while maintaining your focus on the activity of breathing itself the whole time. As you inhale, simply observe the breath coming in, and as you exhale simply notice the breath going out. Your mind should be in a neutral state, impartial, free of judgment. Do not exert your mind; let it rest naturally on the simple activity of breathing. You should repeat this process for as long as you can.

2. No doubt many thoughts will arise, and your mind will begin to drift; as your mind begins to wander, just observe this happening and then bring it back in focus. Take a couple of deep breaths, as explained before, and then direct your attention to your breathing once again.

Initially, you can begin the practice of formal sitting for five to ten minutes. As you progress, and your ability to remain focused on the simple activity of breathing becomes longer, you can gradually increase the length of time of formal sitting.

Exercise B

Some individuals, particularly those with more active minds, may find the first exercise to be a bit difficult, at least in the beginning stages of practice. These individuals may find another variation of the meditation to be more effective. The variation involves counting the breaths in addition to observing the breath. Some people find that counting helps them maintain their attention on the breath. Here, go through the same preparation of body and mind.

1. After taking a couple of deep breaths, direct your attention to your breathing. As before, you should breathe normally,

allowing your breaths to flow in and out effortlessly. Now, instead of simply observing the breaths, you should mentally count your breaths. Count each round of inhalation and exhalation as one unit. So as you inhale and then exhale, mentally count "one," then "two," "three," and so on. Initially, you could count up to ten, fifteen, or twenty-one, depending on how long you can retain your attention without being distracted.

2. As your mind begins to wander, simply note that this is happening and bring it back in focus. Take a couple of deep breaths, as before, and then resume breathing and counting.

Initially, it is better if you keep the session of your sitting relatively short, say five to ten minutes. However, as you make progress in your mental discipline, your ability to remain focused in meditation will increase naturally.

Whichever of the two exercises you may choose to do, it is important to maintain a regular system of practice. The routine and regularity of your practice itself will bring a degree of discipline and focus to your life. As you become familiar with this kind of deliberate, formal sitting exercise, you will gradually acquire the ability to cultivate a settled mental state that you can then successfully direct to any chosen topic. In this way, you will be able to overcome many of the problems that arise simply as a result of an unfocused, undisciplined mental state.

FOR FURTHER INFORMATION

For further information about the Dalai Lama, his other books, and his schedule of teachings and public talks throughout the world, please go to the website: www.dalailama.com.

For further information about Dr. Howard Cutler's workshops, talks, and activities, please go to the website: www.theartofhappiness.com.